DATE			

Varieties and Problems of Twentieth-Century Socialism

Varieties and Problems of Twentieth-Century Socialism

Louis Patsouras
Jack Ray Thomas

Nelson-Hall nh Chicago

Cop. 2

Library of Congress Cataloging in Publication Data

Main entry under title:

Varieties and problems of twentieth-century socialism.

  Bibliography:
  Includes index.
  1. Communism—Addresses, essays, lectures.
  2. Socialism—Addresses, essays, lectures.
  I. Patsouras, Louis   II.   Thomas, Jack Ray.
  HB40.V314   335′.009′04   79-21450
  ISBN 0-88229-444-X (cloth)
  ISBN 0-88229-743-0 (paper)

Manufactured in the United States of America

10 9 8 7 6 5 4 3 2 1

Contents

Preface

Socialism is a subject that has been studied extensively over the last two centuries. This scholarly interest has led to the publication of numerous books and articles. Many of these compositions are of very high quality, but they all approach the subject from a discipline-oriented perspective. Consequently, there are histories of socialism, political examinations of socialism, economic approaches to socialism, but seldom has there been an interdisciplinary study. In discussing this vital force, college teachers usually stress those aspects that are germane to their respective disciplines. This anthology seeks to rectify that deficiency by viewing socialism in a more complete form. It focuses upon socialism's historical impact by way of sociopolitical, philosophical, and artistic-spiritual dimensions. It also presents the various aspects of socialism through the activity and ideas of some of its principal proponents, thereby keeping intact the personal side of the historical equation.

Introduction

Socialism as a way of life and as a philosophy is not new. Elements of it are deeply rooted in the very core of the human ethos. For hundreds of thousands of years, Stone Age man lived in societies characterized by intense mutual aid and solidarity in which little or no labor division existed, general equality prevailed, and where war, if it ever existed, was of only peripheral importance.

The great turning point in history occurred with the several agricultural revolutions that in various phases occupied thousands of years. For example, as early as 10,000 B.C., incipient agriculture was in evidence in sections of the Middle East, but it was not until 3500 B.C. that civilization developed there, undergirded by a maturity that resulted from the agricultural revolution.

With the advent of civilization and a sedentary way of life, there soon developed societies which, with some notable exceptions such as the democracy in classical Hellas, were class-ridden, authoritarian, and dominated by power elites. The agricultural revolution allowed for a substantial enough economic surplus to make profitable the exploitation of man by man. Until recently the traditional pattern of social power rested with the class that possessed military power—the nobility and clerics—and their supporters who controlled the cultural-ideological apparatus. Their hegemony rested on their exploitation of the peasantry; this was the basic characteristic of the slave and manorial society that prevailed in many areas of the world until a few centuries ago. Despite this long-term social oppression, or perhaps because of it, elements of socialism existed, both in the daily lives of the peasantry, as with the collective planting and harvesting carried on by medieval serfs in an atmosphere of extensive mutual aid and in the philosophical-religious realm of various thinkers and religious prophets. In the ancient world, Pythagoras greatly influenced Plato's view of communism as the highest ideal of humanity, while the Hebrew prophets, Micah, Amos, and Isaiah, expounded intense social criticism and lyrical utopianism. Later, during the Middle Ages, St. Francis of Assisi expressed social concern for mankind, and in the Renaissance, Sir Thomas More in his book *Utopia* displayed an advanced social awareness. Gerrard Winstanley in his book *New Laws of Righteousness,* published during the English revolutionary period in the 1640s, and Rousseau in his *Discourse on Origins of Inequality,* which appeared during the Enlightenment, both displayed an understanding of social problems that plagued mankind. Already, before the nineteenth century, these people in a collective sense enunciated such ideals as: (1) the abolition of private exploitative property, (2) a classless society, (3) the end of war, (4) the importance of the individual *qua* individual, and (5) the abolition of government.

With the coming of the Industrial Revolution in the Western world, beginning in the late eighteenth century in Great Britain, the bourgeoisie, which had been in the process of development for centuries, soon became the leading social class, displacing the nobility. The rise of the bourgeoisie, with the coming of the Industrial Revolution, necessarily contributed to the creation and development of a numerous proletariat which quickly challenged the liberal ideas of the bourgeoisie with socialistic views of its own. Not surprisingly the two leading thinkers of socialism, Karl Marx and Pierre Joseph Proudhon, lived in the nineteenth century—the former a leading thinker in the development of twentieth-century democratic socialism and communism; the latter, not only one of the fathers of anarchism, along with Bakunin and Godwin, but also an important figure in democratic socialism and one of the inspirers of anarcho or revolutionary syndicalism. Both Marx and Proudhon evolved a theory of historical development which stressed the class struggle (the proletariat versus the bourgeoisie); the eventual triumph of the proletariat; and a new society which would ultimately be classless and stateless.

By the twentieth century, the ideas of the past began to have a greater impact on nations and peoples. In this atmosphere of growing awareness and amidst the emergence of a variety of philosophies and political theories, socialism became an even greater factor. As problems created by world capitalism intensified, sometimes exacerbated by the rise of socialism itself, it became more apparent that the important role of economic and social planning in the non-Socialist as well as the Socialist sectors of capitalist societies helped stabilize capitalism's periodic economic crises. Nevertheless, capitalism's basic problems were rooted in certain economic propensities, such as imperialism of the modern variety, designed to acquire raw materials and markets, and in its penetration even of independent, economically backward nations. These actions led to periodic economic boom-and-bust cycles which by the Great Depression of the 1930s elicited state intervention in one form or another. Obviously, these economic categories spilled over into the sociopolitical spheres in which socialism was vitally involved.

As capitalism fell on more difficult days in the twentieth century, some of its long-term problems became more unwieldy. One such difficulty was imperialism. In a very real sense, Western imperialism, which has existed for the last four hundred years, is intimately tied to the rise of capitalism from its early merchant-capital phase in the fifteenth to eighteenth centuries to its finance-capital phase in the twentieth century. This imperialism was decisive in insuring the continued economic backwardness of its victims—those people who were colonized. Even in independent, economically backward nations such as Imperial Russia, Western economic penetration brought about certain acute sociopolitical problems. Generally, the nations of the two preceding categories suffered a deformed economic development being forced into a subordinate economic role—relegated to raw material industries and/or tied to the finance capital of advanced nations—that prevented overall economic development so necessary for a nation to progress into the modern technological age. (Japan is an exception to this type of development because she herself became imperialistic.)

Western imperialism did not sufficiently alter the sociopolitical authoritarianism imbedded in the traditional rural society which it dominated. In fact, the proletariat that did develop under its impact in Russia and China was so alienated that it fell under the influence of socialism. Moreover, imperialism was important in the development of rival national blocs in international politics, a factor of some importance in generating World Wars I and II. As a result of the first world conflict, along with other causes, Russia, which was the weak link in European capitalism, in 1917 became the first socialist nation in history. Its socialism (communism), which obviously reflected the Russian authoritarian past, set about, as its first priority, to industrialize the nation and thereby make her the equal of Western powers. Later, imperialism became a fundamental part of the German experience. The great world depression of the 1930s was predicated in part on the fact that a strong German Left existed which was a threat to the traditional capitalist structure in time of economic crises. Nazism, among other things, represented an aggressive economic nationalism bent on imperialistic expansion and, consequently, it was one of the main causes that brought about World War II. Nazism also included racism and aggressive nationalism, two of the more despicable aspects of imperialism, which are generally inextricably intertwined. The Nazi plan for a master race to exploit Europe and the world with their allies was not merely a parody of imperialism but its ultimate quintessence.

World War II so completely vitiated Western and Japanese imperialism that within China, communism emerged as the dominant political ideology. To be sure, the adverse affects of Japanese occupation, and the fact that traditional Chinese society and political structures were already in the process of disintegration under the impact of Western and Japanese imperialism, also contributed to communism's triumph in that nation. Meanwhile, British rule ended in India and within a generation the remainder of British colonialism collapsed along with that of the French, Dutch, Belgian, and Portuguese. Into this void stepped Arab socialism in Algeria, Egypt, Iraq, and Syria; Black socialism in Angola, Mozambique, Tanzania, and Kenya, and, in the Orient, Vietnamese communism. In addition, socialism in Europe achieved significant gains. Eastern Europe fell under the sway of the Soviet Communists, while, in Western Europe, extensive programs of nationalization in industry and finance occurred in Great Britain, France and Italy. Even West Germany became involved in nationalization as its Federal and state governments took control of about twenty precent of the share capital of its industry.

In summary, socialism, in one form or another, has by this last quarter of the twentieth century come to guide the destinies of a large share of the world's population. As a result it is necessary to look more closely at the major types of socialism so influential in every area of the globe.

As socialism developed in the twentieth century it moved in three different major streams: (1) anarchism and its derivative, anarcho and/or revolutionary syndicalism; (2) democratic socialism found mainly in Western Europe; and (3) communism, which is an authoritarian socialism dominant in the Soviet Union, the Chinese People's Republic, and Vietnam.

These three brands of socialism are all distinct but they do have some common features. For example, all three believe in the class struggle. For Communist anarchism, which is the main contemporary Anarchist type, as well as for communism and such Marxian Socialist parties as the Italian Socialist party, the Spanish Socialist party, the French Socialist party, and, to an extent, the German Social Democratic party, the basic sociopolitical and cultural struggle is essentially between those who own the means of production and of exchange and those who work for the owners. Obviously, there are many nuances in this framework based on bourgeois-proletarian polarity—religion, nationalism, imperialism, and the rural-urban configuration—which make for complexity in any attempt to understand it. Also, a part of the peasantry became embroiled in wars of national liberation against imperialism or were unionized on large estates, becoming a part of the international proletariat. The class struggle in the industrialized West, where democratic traditions took hold by the late nineteenth century, was of a pragmatic and evolutionary nature. The idea of the peaceful advent of socialism was attractive, but, in the economically backward areas of Russia and China the lack of a democratic experience, which in a real sense reflected the social rigidity of economic underdevelopment, dictated revolution and civil war as hallmarks of change. Not surprisingly, communism in the contemporary period in Russia and China is totalitarian and, therefore, not tolerant of opposing ideologies. Yet, a dissonant note has come from the French and Italian Communist parties, which are far more tolerant of new and different ideas and accept democracy. These differences, however, are of recent vintage and do not alter the basic agreement of most Socialists on the concept of class struggle.

The three main types of socialism also agreed upon the Socialist vision. This concept holds that class societies founded on the private ownership of the means of production and exchange by privileged groups of capitalists for a society where property is of a collective nature should be terminated. Moreover, they agree that within a period of time, a classless and stateless society will emerge.

While these areas of agreement exist there is no uniformity among the types of socialism. Within these movements, especially the large mass ones in different areas of the world, the level of socioeconomic development coupled with past social struggles have conspired to create considerable differences among Socialist nations and Socialist parties. For example, in Vietnam, communism was more intimately tied to the nationalism associated with national liberation from French colonialism and United States imperialism than it was to the war communism phase (1918-1921) of Russian communism, in which proletarian internationalism occupied center stage. Keeping such differences in mind, it is possible to delineate the essentials of the three main Socialist streams in a coherent manner.

Of the various principal streams of socialism, anarchism may be regarded as the most utopian. Its Promethean vision of the world posits the end of all authority immediately with the coming of socialism. Upon the completion of a successful Socialist revolution over the bourgeoisie, Anarchists insist that a classless and stateless society must be created at once.

The stateless society would emerge with the overturn of the bourgeoisie and the immediate disestablishment of its state apparatus: army, police courts, and civil bureaucracy. Into the breach a decentralized society would step, one guided basically by local (on a geographical basis) committees drawn from the general population. Participatory democracy would be involved in all areas of collective human endeavor.

Classlessness would soon develop as well. With the abolition of private exploitative property and the end of a wage system, man's work would not be confined within the rather narrow economic dimensions of the present. In addition, Anarchists would set up a general pattern of culture which would, within a reasonable period of time, create a society of technical-cultural equals in which the worker-management syndrome would not exist and in which labor division as we now know it would become a relic of the past.

Anarchism evolved a model for change which includes the support of piecemeal pragmatic reform within the confines of democratic society as it is now constituted, viewing the cumulative reforms as a basis for the final change which would result from a general strike. Anarchism's classic century was the nineteenth, when its leading thinkers flourished. Men like William Godwin, Pierre-Joseph Proudhon, and Michael Bakunin caught the fancy of many intellectuals and workers alike with their arguments. Later, in the twentieth century, a new generation of ideologues headed by Peter Kropotkin and Jean Grave continued the work of their predecessors. Additionally, anarchism attracted many artists and intellectuals over the years, such as Percy Bysshe Shelley, Leo Tolstoy, and Henry David Thoreau. At the end of the nineteenth century, anarchism had a vast following among those in the world of art and intellectuality.

Although of lesser importance than democratic socialism and communism in twentieth-century socialism, anarchism has, nevertheless, contributed significantly to socialism's success. It was an important force in the Spanish Socialist stream, participating honorably and valiantly in the 1936 Spanish Civil War.

The greatest influence of anarchism, however, has been in the labor movement. Anarchist militants, especially in France and Spain, entered the union movement to help in transforming a part of it into a revolutionary organization whose purpose was to destroy bourgeois society through a series of strikes that would ultimately grow into a crippling general strike. The unions then would form the nucleus of the new Socialist society, organizing and administering not only industrial production but the various civil functions of the state. This anarchist ideal forms the basis of anarcho and/or revolutionary syndicalism. The French and Spanish labor confederations of the twentieth century have held firmly to these concepts.

In recent social developments, Anarchist ideology influenced the French Rebellion of 1968, when student strikes and street battles with the police sparked numerous other walkouts that soon led to a general strike that almost ended the status quo in France. This and other minor successes strengthened the Anarchist perspective of the methods necessary to bring about change in a mature capitalist society that is partially Socialist.

Communism is a type of socialism that is basically associated with former economically underdeveloped nations, like Russia, and with developing ones, notably the Chinese People's Republic. In both of these countries, communism gained power through a period of revolution in a backdrop of war which helped soften the fabric of the former political structures. Marxian socialism is the dominant theme of these societies but they inordinately stress its authoritarian elements such as the dictatorship of the proletariat. This authoritarian model of socialism developed in nations where principles of freedom, which slowly developed over the past centuries in the bourgeois West, were unknown. Instead, these nations were ruled by a reactionary autocracy—tsarism in Russia, imperial government in China. Both nations failed to develop a sizable bourgeoisie and industrial proletariat, although it was the proletariat of Russia which spearheaded its communism, while in China, communism triumphed through its alliance with a revolutionary peasantry. (The Marxian prediction that socialism would first come in the industrialized Western nations through a politically conscious working class proved false. Instead, socialism has come to power in nations whose social fabric was so weakened by war and imperialism that it was able to capitalize on mass popular discontent.)

Twentieth-century communism is basically Marxian in character, although it has hyphenated Marx's name with that of Lenin's in Russia and has added Mao's to the two in China. Although authoritarianist in nature, the Communist goal is for a society along Anarchist lines, a stateless and classless society devoid of authority. For the Communists, however, this cannot be done immediately following a successful socialist revolution, but must await such stages and events as the establishment of socialism throughout the world and a generally much higher level of techno-productive and cultural development than is now existent.

The center of twentieth-century democratic socialism is in the non-Communist part of Europe. Democratic socialism fits well into the patterns of life and politics developed especially in Western Europe and Scandinavia, where social conflict has been to a large degree confined within a democratic framework. These countries have proven fertile ground for socialism also because of their industrial maturity coupled with political structures that have been amenable to progressive socioeconomic and political change during the last hundred or so years. There are, of course, exceptions to this, notably the Nazi period in Germany (1933-1945) and the Italian Fascist period of the 1920s and 1930s; but as one looks at the non-Communist European historical panorama at least from the perspective of the mid-1970s, it seems that the forces of democracy are in the ascendancy, so much so that the two leading Communist parties in Western Europe—the French and Italian—appear now well on their way to accepting the democratic path to socialism.

In any discussion of European democratic socialism, special mention should be made of the German Social Democratic party, the French Socialist party, and the British Labor party. The German Social Democratic party, for much of its history, has been reformist and Marxian. However, in the last decade or two, much of the Marxian rhetoric has been toned down or eliminated. This party had and still has a large electoral following and has played a significant role in twentieth-century German history.

The French Socialist party is heir to a long-standing French revolutionary tradition and ideologically has been most influenced by the ideas of Jean Jaures, whose Socialist philosophy was eclectic, combining the views of various thinkers including those of Karl Marx. Jaurès' disciple, Léon Blum, was the premier of France in 1936-1937 during the hectic Popular Front period in which Communists, Socialists, and Radicals combined electorally to defeat a potential Fascist threat. The party has been active and influential since the Popular Front days.

Finally, the British Labor party is a Socialist group formed by middle-class intellectuals who early in this century organized the Fabian Society. It includes some other minor Socialist groups and British labor unions which comprise its mass electoral base. The party has always been pragmatic and cautious in its approach to the establishment of socialism.

The similarities and differences noted among the three main Socialist movements have allowed for both conflict and cooperation in their relations with each other. For example, the current Soviet-Chinese national-ideological dispute, which has been exacerbated by different levels of economic development and proximity to the experience of revolution, has been a problem for the entire socialist world. Less crucial but equally frustrating for Socialists has been the increasing departure from Soviet guidance of Western Communist parties. While ideologically these elements are in basic agreement, they differ widely on practical measures and sometimes dissipate their energies in lengthy, sometimes bitter, quarrels. But such activity is not new to the Socialist world. Indeed, a major characteristic of the Socialist movement has been its diversity.

Generally, after the successful Communist revolution of November 1917 in Russia, relations between revolutionary Communists and reformist-democratic Socialists were severely strained for about a decade and a half, because the Russian Communists, in their drive to power, destroyed the various non-Communist Socialist groups in Russia. However, after the rise of fascism in Italy and nazism in Germany, the Communists in the mid-thirties successfully achieved a Popular Front with the Democratic Socialists and progressive middle-class groups in France and Spain. The basic aim of this loose coalition was to stop further Fascist inroads. Cooperation between the Democratic Socialists and Communists continued during World War II, notably in France and Italy, where both groups were popular. Then, even with the advent of the Cold War between Soviet communism and Western liberal democracy in which the Democratic Socialist parties chose the democratic West over the authoritarianism of the Communists, electoral pacts and common programs in France and Italy between

Communists and Democratic Socialists (despite periods of coldness) continued and are in evidence in the mid-seventies.

The Anarchists have not had the most pleasant relations with their two stronger rivals. With respect to communism it is true that in the early days of Communist rule in Russia many Western Anarchists supported it, but in consolidating their rule their authoritarianism became ever more manifest as they destroyed the Socialist opposition—including the Anarchist part. The Anarchists have consistently criticized Soviet rule, pointing out that its disregard for elementary civil liberties—freedom of speech and press—is a betrayal of socialism. In the Spanish Civil War period of 1936-1939, the Communists, with the Spanish Socialists, broke Anarchist power in Catalonia in the summer of 1937. With the Democratic Socialists, despite Anarchist revolutionary proclivities, there developed a strong pragmatic stance in much of the Anarchist thought. This, coupled with the fact that Democratic Socialists are staunch defenders of civil liberties, allowed for peaceful relations between the two except for Anarchist terrorist groups.

On the whole, then, the different brands of socialism have worked together on occasion but have also found themselves at odds in some instances. Their cooperation has been beneficial to all concerned, and their conflicts, while sometimes bitter, have not been rancorous enough as yet to cause serious difficulty within the total Socialist world. Indeed, differences of opinion and varying interpretations of doctrine are a healthy facet of a vital, expansive socialism.

While politically there has been both friendship and antagonism among the various Socialist elements, intellectuals from all groups have espoused the concept that the arts may be used to enhance Socialist ideology and, at the same time, disseminate the Socialist message throughout the world. In the understanding of the twentieth-century Socialist condition, its enrichment by the world of art is extremely significant. Indeed, in the very ethos of socialism, the matter of art is of crucial importance. The Socialist quest for justice, equality, and fraternity, and to replace a world with varying degrees of inequality, injustice, and the attendant alienation, has a significant artistic-spiritual dimension that could not but attract many artists, people who by their very natures are at once the most creative and sensitive. As Peter Kropotkin, the prominent Anarcho-Communist has written, under anarchism everyone will be an artist because anarchism itself represents art.

There is an extensive tradition with respect to socialism and its connections with the world of art. In the nineteenth century, a concerted onslaught against the status quo was launched by a major segment of the Romantic movement, as well as by some of its various offshoots. Romanticism, with its pervasive Promethean spirit (with the individual defying all social conventions and authority), in conjunction with a rising equalitarian spirit, brought forth such socialist artists as Shelley, Sand, Ibsen, and Tolstoy.

In the twentieth century, the attack among artists against the forces of power, both bourgeois and Communist, has continued. George Orwell, Andre Malraux, Jean-Paul Sartre, Albert Camus, and Nikos Kazantzakis have waged their struggle through the printed page. To a significant degree, these writers either included Socialist themes in their works and/or wrestled with various aspects which included socialism in their views of the twentieth-century human condition. Their contributions to Socialist thought and propagation cannot be ignored.

The following study deals first with the principal Socialist movements of the twentieth century: democratic socialism is explored through the lives of Léon Blum and Salvador Allende, anarchism is highlighted in the study on Jean Grave (Peter Kropotkin's leading disciple), and communism is examined in the articles on Georgi Dimitrov and Ho Chi Minh. Following these initial explorations into socialism, the study focuses on some of the basic problems of the twentieth-century Socialist complex. These include the relationship of Marxism and democracy as examined in the work of Lucio Colletti, the prominent Italian political theorist. Next, the issue of individual freedom, as seen through the ideas of Erich Fromm, one of the leading Socialist philosophers of our century, is attacked. Finally, attention is given to the connection between socialism and art, using the encounter with socialism of the prominent novelist, Nikos Kazant-zakis, a writer important in delineating the human condition of the twentieth century.

The editors recognize that not all types of socialism can be incorporated into one book of this nature, nor can we include all the major theoreticians and political leaders. Instead, we have had to choose the most prominent phases of socialism and men who reflect major Socialist attitudes. The list includes people who have led nations and had an input on world politics, in addition to those who have wielded no political power but whose thoughts have served as inspiration for multitudes of people. Some suc-ceeded in their immediate goals while others failed, but all made contributions to the great body of Socialist literature. Conse-quently, we believe that an acquaintance with the figures included in this book and familiarity with their ideas will enable the reader to understand better the Socialist phenomenon, if only by recog-nizing its diversity.

Chapter 1

Democratic Socialism

Léon Blum and Democratic Socialism in France

by Louis Patsouras

Léon Blum was the foremost Democratic Socialist on the world scene between World War I and World War II. Not only was he involved in day-to-day politics as a member of the French Chamber of Deputies, but, at a critical point in history, he became the first Socialist premier of France (1936-1937) and the symbol of the Popular Front—a coalition of Socialists, Communists, and Radical Socialists. Throughout his political career, Blum played an important role in maintaining French democracy while pushing for socialism.

Léon Blum is one of the significant Socialists and statesmen of the twentieth century. Indeed, in the period between World Wars I and II, he was the outstanding Democratic Socialist in Europe, not only serving as the first Socialist premier of France in the first Popular Front ministry of 1936-1937, but also contributing significantly to Socialist thought. This remarkable man, born in Paris in April, 1872, came from a Jewish bourgeois background that had known recent poverty and was also involved in socialism: Blum's father, Auguste, overcame penury by establishing with his brothers a prosperous wholesale ribbon establishment, while the Socialist influence came from his maternal grandmother, Henriette Picart, who owned a bookstore in Paris. A member of the Left, she wholeheartedly supported the Paris Commune of 1871, the greatest European working-class revolution in the nineteenth century.

3

Blum was a precocious youngster; he excelled scholastically at the Lycée Charlemagne and the Lycée Henri IV in Paris. In 1890, he entered the École Normale Supérieure, a prestigious school for teachers. While there he was introduced to the ideas of Marx by Lucien Herr, the school librarian, who was instrumental in spreading Marxism among the school's intellectual elite. Blum's stay was not of long duration; he was forced to leave in 1891 after failing some examinations. Soon afterward, Blum entered the Sorbonne, where he received degrees in literature and in law. In 1895, Blum gained entrance to the Council of State (something like a Supreme Court to which cases between citizens and government involving administrative law are referred). Blum advanced steadily in this civil service situation to become finally *commissaire du gouvernement,* where he used his vast legal experience to inform the court of the various intricacies of law with respect to cases tried before it. He worked for the Council of State until 1919, when he entered the lower house of the French Parliament, the Chamber of Deputies.[1]

For some years, Blum was on the fringes of French socialism. Although sympathetic to it, he was not as yet definitely committed. In 1896, his friend Herr introduced Blum to Jean Jaurès, the great French Socialist leader of the period. Soon, they formed a lasting friendship which was important in Blum's becoming a Socialist: Blum always considered himself a disciple of Jaurès.[2]

In 1897, Herr convinced Blum that Captain Alfred Dreyfus of the French army, an Alsatian Jew, had been unjustly condemned to Devil's Island for allegedly selling military secrets to Germany. The case was one where anti-Semitism was significant. Sections of the upper bourgeoisie and nobility, important circles in the Catholic church, and an important part of the military, where royalism and antirepublicanism reigned, were determined to continue the frame-up. Supporting Dreyfus were liberal and Socialist groups, which were staunch republicans. Blum became a Dreyfusard (a defender of Dreyfus) and belonged to practically all the important groups that demanded justice for him. This case thoroughly politicized Blum and made him a lifelong and dedicated Socialist.[3] In 1899 Blum became a formal member of the Groupe de l'Unité Socialiste (Group for Socialist Unity).

Complementing his legal work and indeed occurring parallel with his introduction to socialism was Blum's literary activity, in which he excelled to the point of emerging as one of France's leading literary critics as a member of the staff of *La Revue Blanche* (White Review), a leading literary journal in the pre-World War I generation. The journal's milieu, basically Anarchist in political orientation, influenced him to where he became sympathetic to anarchism: an 1892 Blum article in the journal praising anarchism is ample proof of this. Anarchism, however, was just a passing fancy—Blum was an idealist, but as one deeply involved with government, he could not basically be receptive to this sort of socialism.

Blum's early ideas concerning socialism and the human condition are contained in *Nouvelles Conversations de Goethe avec Eckermann* (New Conversations of Goethe with Eckermann), 1901, where the great German writer, Goethe, author of *Dr. Faustus* (who represents man's wrestling with knowledge and evil), has a series of imaginary conversations with one of his disciples, Eckermann. Goethe (Blum) a democratic and humanistic Socialist has Faust (his alter ego) becoming a Socialist whose aim is to "impose justice on humanity"[4] peacefully, while Mephistopheles, also a Socialist (sometimes the friend of Faust and sometimes his rival) is for violence and revenge against the bourgeoisie. Blum already was for a peaceful reformist socialism that would lessen the shock between a militant socialism and the bourgeoisie in order that the collectivization of property might be done without recourse to violence.

In 1902, Blum finally joined Jaurès's Socialist party, the Parti Socialiste Français. In 1905, this group joined with the Parti Socialiste de France, a Marxian party, to form the Parti Socialiste, Section Française de l'Internationale Ouvrière. The unity was imposed by the Second Socialist International (1889-1914) which insisted that in order to strengthen socialism the revolutionary Marxists and Democratic Socialists should lay aside differences for the greater strength of unity.[5]

Although a Socialist militant, Blum, because of his intense activity in the Council of State and as literary critic, did not heed Jaurès's pleas to run as representative to the Chamber of Dep-

uties. To be sure, for a while in 1904 and 1905, Blum was part
of the staff of the great Socialist daily *l'Humanité* that was founded
in 1904 by Jaurès. However, in 1905, he left it after its content
became less literary and more concerned with fulfilling the needs
of the average Socialist. (Blum was to write in the decade before 1914 his significant work concerning literary criticism, *Sten-
dhal et le Beylisme,* and the socio-psychological *Du Marriage* (Of
ᴀᴠɴ rriage), which advocated—even for women—a period of sex-
ual experimentation before marriage.)[6] Blum's activity with respect to socialism, after the brief flurry with *l'Humanité* until his
running for deputy as a Socialist in 1919, was basically centered
on the meetings, which he attended regularly, of his party's section—the Fourteenth of Paris. Blum's metamorphosis with respect to becoming a dedicated Socialist, where he decided that
he would one day devote much of his time to it, came about with
the assassination of his friend Jean Jaurès in July 1914.[7] The
noted literary critic was to become a dedicated Socialist activist.

World War I proved to be a traumatic experience for French
and international socialism. The Second Socialist International
was aware of the fact that various international crises might bring
war, and it evolved a strategy to meet them. At its 1912 Basel
Congress, the problem of war, for example, was of primary concern. The delegates resolved to pay constant attention to the
dangers of war and to maintain close communications among the
various Socialist parties with respect to it. It was further resolved
that "the fear of the ruling classes of a proletarian revolution,
which would occur immediately with a world war, was an essential guarantee to peace."[8] When war seemed imminent in the middle of July, 1914, the French Socialists called for an extraordinary congress that was held in Paris (July 14-16), which was
attended by Socialist delegates of many nations. The majority
of the congress, including Jaurès, approved a resolution that demanded an international general strike of the proletariat to prevent
the holocaust of war. Jaurès, especially worked feverishly for
peace, declaring in a July 25 speech at Lyons:

> The workers of France, England, Germany, and Italy, those
> countless thousands of men and women, must unite. Their hearts
> must beat as one to prevent this horrible disaster.[9]

Following a committee meeting of the Second International at Brussels that was held on July 29 to discuss means of preventing war, Jaurès returned to Paris, hopeful that this was possible. All was in vain, however, as he was assassinated by a nationalist fanatic on July 31. Within a few days the great European nations had launched World War I.

Socialism was impotent before the fires of war. And, once war began, most Socialists supported the war effort of their respective governments—Blum falls into this category. He tried to join the army, but was rejected because of nearsightedness. When the French Socialists sent two of their prominent members, Jules Guesde and Marcel Sembat, to serve as ministers on the war cabinet of the René Viviani government, Blum joined Sembat as his executive secretary. In this capacity, Blum played a considerable part in the war effort. His responsible position brought him into intimate contact with the multifarious problems of governmental administration, which in turn aided the future premier to gain new insights concerning politics and government. In a brilliant essay, "La Réforme gouvernementale," which appeared anonymously in the prestigious bourgeois journal *La Revue de Paris* in 1918 (the anonymity was probably connected to the leftward trend in French socialism during the period, which the reformist Blum had to be wary of), Blum clearly and cogently presented the critical problems of governmental administration and the role of political parties with respect to it.) Of primordial importance was the French need for a more powerful and stable premiership:

> In a democratic state, sovereignty in theory belongs to the people and to the assembly which represents it. But in practice it is delegated to one person. Necessity wished it thus. It is just as necessary to have a head in government as it is to have one in industry.[10]

The second major problem, one which would ultimately allow for Socialist cooperation in a coalition Popular Front ministry, was participation in government at the proper time:

> Parliamentary life is a preparation for the entire subject of government; it teaches, or it must teach the elements of law, of legislation, and of the national economy.[11]

On the problem of governmental stability, one which had constantly plagued France for many years, Blum asserted that it could come about only by a better organization of French political parties, which, with a concrete program of action, would insure stable premierships.[12]

The basic reformism just enunciated was to run into the determined opposition of Socialist revolutionary groups that not only opposed what they considered a capitalist war, but which urged that the war itself be used as a base to launch a Socialist revolution. At first, the revolutionary Socialists were a miniscule minority in France and other European nations, but in their two international congresses held during World War I in Switzerland—at Zimmerwald in September 1915 and at Kienthal in April 1916— they indicated determined opposition to war. By the latter congress, the resolution of V. I. Lenin, the chief figure of revolutionary Russian socialism, that the war be used as a launching pad for a worldwide Socialist revolution was adopted by the majority. This seemed academic, however, until 1917, when Russia (the strains of war were too much for the backward semifeudal tsarist government) experienced two revolutions in 1917, in March and November. In the second, the revolutionary Bolsheviks under Lenin seized power and called for revolution against war and capitalism. The carnage of World War I in which millions of combatants were killed and wounded, and its seemingly endless duration, in addition to the Bolshevik triumph in Russia, strengthened and emboldened the revolutionary side of socialism throughout the world. In French socialism, for example, as early as July 1918, the majority, although upholding the right of national defense, called for an immediate peace without winners or losers and declared that international Socialist solidarity was of prime importance. Furthermore, they were against Socialist participation in a bourgeois war government. Blum, in the minority, had held the opinion that the French Socialists should continue to exercise an active role in a government of national defense in order to serve the higher interests of the proletariat: to keep watch on Georges Clemenceau's (Premier of France from November 1917 to January 1920) anti-labor attitude, and to press for Socialist participation in future deliberations concerning peace proposals and conferences.[13]

The end of World War I in November 1918, and the formation of the Third (Communist) International in March 1919 led to the further radicalization of French socialism. Blum, during this period, tried to effect a compromise between the Bolshevik-oriented left wing led by Marcel Cachin and others, and the right wing led by such men as Albert Thomas, a former minister of munitions during World War I, and Marcel Sembat, who were basically reformists. The left wing, however, was to soon make demands that for the reformists were unacceptable, thereby splitting French socialism.

In December 1920, the most significant congress in the history of French socialism occurred in Tours—its repercussions are still felt today as it resulted in the division of French socialism into two great rival parties, the reformist Socialists and revolutionary Communists. The Communist International had presented, just prior to the congress, twenty-one demands that French socialism had to accept before joining it.[14] Among the primary ones were: (1) the demand that French socialism accept the principle of the dictatorship of the proletariat, (2) the demand for centralization and iron discipline within the party, (14) the demand that the new Communist party to be formed was obligated to defend the Soviet Union, and (21) the demand for the removal of all those not agreeing with the preceding twenty demands.

After the congress had decided to join the Communist International by a 3,208 to 1,022 vote with 397 abstentions (Blum abstained), it was ordered by the Communist International to expel moderates such as Marcel Sembat and Albert Thomas. Blum was not mentioned, but his close ties to Sembat and his opposition to the twenty-one demands virtually assured that he would be one of those purged. Blum was now in determined opposition to the Communist International, and with Sembat and others proposed that the Socialists not join it. This proposal lost by 3,247 to 1,398 votes. French socialism was then irrevocably split into rival Socialist and Communist parties. Blum voiced his ultimate opposition to the twenty-one demands in this manner:

> Do you believe that a majority vote can change the state of my conscience? Because so many votes are for and so many votes against, do you believe that the state of my reason and of my heart toward a problem like that would change itself?[15]

In 1919, Blum decided to become active in parliamentary life, and was successful in his bid to be elected to the Chamber of Deputies. After the split at Tours, he soon emerged as an outstanding personality of the Socialist party, becoming its president in 1924. The principal tasks which he faced were to delineate the theoretical differences vis-à-vis the Communists and to rebuild the shattered Socialist party.

With respect to Blum's defense of socialism and criticism of communism, he followed the reformist pattern of thought laid down by Jaurès. In a brilliant polemical pamphlet published in 1928, *Bolchevisme et socialisme,* Blum proclaimed his faith that French socialism could successfully transform by gradual change the present bourgeois society by working within its democratic framework:

> And we have always persisted in our thinking that the taking of political power, considered uniquely, is not the social revolution. That, on the contrary, it does not create the Revolution or become the revolution than in the measure where the proletariat, the depository of power, can use it to implant a new form of property. We then conclude that the real revolutionary preparation consists in leading the transformation of the social complex rather than in arming ourselves for a showdown; and we will put the working class on guard against any premature or unwise moves.[16]

In Blum's view, socialism would come about only after a mature society had decided democratically. Only then, if the bourgeoisie did not surrender peacefully the totality of its power— a distinct possibility—would Blum envisage dictatorship of the proletariat:

> These periods of legal vacation are by definition periods of dictatorship. The Republican revolutions of the nineteenth century had their instruments of dictatorship, which they called provisional government. It may be that a social revolution would find itself face to face with the same practical necessity and that is why we see in the dictatorship of the proletariat an almost inevitable corollary of a working class revolution.[17]

Blum also asserted that the insistence of the Communists on the necessity of a violent political revolution had forced them into the position of limiting their membership to an elite of revolutionary shock troops under a hierarchical structure of democratic centralism. On the other hand, the Socialists were open in their membership, democratic and not hierarchical, with a party structure, insuring the leadership's responsiveness to the rank and file. He therefore attacked the Communist party:

> Obsessed by the memory of the political revolutions of the nineteenth century it considers also the conquest of power as the essential and unique goal. Under the influence of this past, it refuses to conceive revoltuion under other aspects than those of violence and insurrection.[18]

To be sure, it would be erroneous to assert that Blum's ideology was devoid of any revolutionary content:

> We have always professed that the social transformation, that is to say the revolution, cannot be accomplished without the proletariat having at first conquered the totality of political power. This conquest of power by the proletariat is the necessary condition of the revolution, precisely because the new society, which will be the fruit of revolutionary activity, will differ in its essence from the present society.[19]

The essential philosophic difference in the polemic between Blum and communism seemed to be in their "mystique" toward revolution. For the Communists, the revolution in and of itself was the supreme justification, whereas for the Socialists it was subordinate to the will of the majority of the people.

After the disaster of Tours, which saw the majority Communists take most of the party's assets, including the important paper, *l'Humanité,* the Socialists slowly recovered. A new official party paper was created—*Le Populaire* ("The Populace"). From 1921 to 1924 Blum was one of its political directors. Publication was suspended in 1925, resuming again in 1927, whereupon it appeared again with Blum as principal figure in its concoction. After Tours, the two great parties of French Socialism—the Socialists and the Communists—competed for members, votes, and parliamentary representation. In every one of these categories (until after World War II) the Socialists far outdistanced their Communist rivals. In party membership, the Socialists, who had been left with only 30,000 after the Tours split increased to about 120,000 by the early 1930s, while their Communist opponents, who started with 120,000, dropped to about 30,000 in the same period. In the 1928 elections (rather representative of the late

1920s and 1930s), Socialists captured 101 of 612 deputies in the Chamber of Deputies and had 1.7 million votes (18 percent), while the Communists elected only 13 deputies with just over one million votes (11 percent).

In the political spectrum, the Socialists were situated between the Communists, to their left, and the Radical Socialists (Radicals), to their right. With respect to the former, the Socialists in the 1920s had bitter relations, though this was to change later in the Popular Front period. For example, after the Socialists refused to cooperate with the Communists in an electoral alliance for the 1928 elections, the Communists pressed their tactic of "class against class,"[20] which was characterized by their refusal to back in the second round of voting Socialist candidates who had more first round votes than Communists. (In the 1924 elections, the Communists supported Socialist candidates while the Socialists did not reciprocate.) With the latter, the Socialists had relatively satisfactory relations. Their ideological differences were great enough to preclude the bitter squabbles of close ideological rivals who shared many common points. Despite the fact that the Radicals were a middle-class party, they did share with the reformist Socialists some common traditions and outlooks: both emphasized the democratic process with respect to change, both were anticlerical, and both were against big business. In the 1924 elections there was an electoral alliance between the two; and when the Radicals emerged as the leading party and formed a government under Edouard Herriot, the Socialists supported them but did not accept any cabinet posts. Under Blum, the majority of the Socialist party was against participation in bourgeois governments unless there were extraordinary circumstances. A major legislative proposal which separated the two parties was indirect taxation—the Radicals for, the Socialists against.[21]

With the Great Depression of the 1930s and the advent of Hitler's rise to power in 1933, which reinforced the Fascist danger already in power in Italy, the French working and lower middle classes decided to form an electoral alliance to bring about social reform and to defend the nation against indigenous quasi-military Fascist groups. The key event that spurred the movement for defense against fascism were the February 6, 1934, riots in Paris, where various quasi-military Fascist groups, including the young Patriots, the Cross of Fire, and others, attacked the Chamber of Deputies in order to force the resignation of Premier Edouard Daladier. Daladier was a Radical, whose party was deeply implicated in covering up a pawnshop scandal which involved some of its prominent members.[22] To meet this Fascist danger, Socialist and Communist unions called a twenty-four-hour general strike for February 12. Communist and Socialist demonstrators on that day were friendly toward one another; for the first time since the split at Tours, Socialists and Communists were acting together.[23] The Communist party of the Soviet Union played down revolutionarism after Hitler's rise to power in 1933 and urged cooperation by all Socialists and liberal groups against Nazism. The Russians wanted a strong and united French ally in case of German attack.[24] The Socialists, sensing the Fascist danger, despite misgivings by Blum and others, joined with the Communists in a "unity of action" pact (July 27, 1934) that was directed against war and fascism.[25] By June 1935, the Radicals had also joined the other two parties. Thus it was that, by June 1935, the Communists, Socialists, and Radical Socialists formed the Popular Front. Among other proposals, these groups decided in the common program to (1) disarm the quasi-military Fascist leagues; (2) respect academic neutrality and secularization; (3) nationalize war industries, such as munitions, in order to take the profit out of war; (4) support the League of Nations and work for peace; (5) restore consumer purchasing power by inaugurating a public-works program for the unemployed; (6) work for a more equitable tax structure based on progressive income taxation; and (7) reform the Bank of France, transforming it from a power base for bankers to a public institution serving all of the people.[26]

The general elections in the spring of 1936 brought the Popular Front a majority of the vote and into power. Blum, in June of 1936, became the first Socialist premier of France; his first premiership lasted until June of 1937.

It was soon obvious that the Popular Front could not undertake fundamental reforms to reconstruct society, obliged as it was to operate within the confines of a basic capitalistic framework and to contend with the presence of the Radicals, who were for

only a limited amount of reform. But, in spite of the many limitations imposed on Blum's first Popular Front government, the
scope of reform undertaken was the most extensive since August
4, 1789. Indeed, the most important reforms were passed in the
first few months of his ministry. Their rapid passage was at least
partially due to the significant strike wave, including many sit-
down strikes, which started in the Paris area on May 26, and
which within ten days involved over a million workers. Although
the capitalists in the well-known Matignon Agreement of June
7, 1936, made many concessions to the workers (protection from
arbitary work dismissal, higher wages, etc.), the strike wave was
so great that it did not end until a week later.[27] On June 9, in
a notable speech before the Chamber, Blum proposed that legislation providing for the forty-hour week, paid annual vacations,
and collective bargaining be passed for the benefit of the working
class. The abolition of the 1935 Laval decrees, which had reduced salaries and pensions of government workers and disabled
war veterans, was also requested. After rapidly passing the Chamber by a huge majority, these proposals were passed by the
Senate after Blum politely reminded them with a touch of irony
of the sit-down strikes that had occurred a short time before.[28]

At the same time, the danger of the Fascist leagues, which
had caused so much trouble on February 6, 1934, was partly
removed when they were dissolved by decree on June 18, fulfilling another part of the Popular Front platform. Furthermore,
the Popular Front simultaneously undertook reform that sought to
democratize the financial powers of the nation and to restrict the
machinations of the financial oligarchy that controlled much of
the nation's life through the Bank of France, the most important
financial institution in the country. Not only was the Bank of
France the custodian of the French gold reserve, it was also a
determinant factor in the expansion and contraction of the nation's economic life by its control of the discount rate. This bank
was run by its Regency Council, controlled by about a dozen of
France's most wealthy families. By the Bank of France Reform
Law of July 25, 1936, the basic power of decision in formulating
policy was diffused among representatives of government, labor,
agriculture, and various business organizations.[29] On August 11,

1936, another milestone was reached, with the passage of a law giving the state the power to nationalize any industry engaged primarily in war production. But due to economic difficulties, nationalization proceeded slowly.[30]

Other reforms affected small farmers, small business, and the unemployed. For the first group, a national Wheat Office was established, which regulated wheat prices and provided for the storage and the exportation of unused wheat. Also under the auspices of the Wheat Office, there was a loan agency to provide farmers with extensive credit. For small businesses, credit facilities were greatly extended. For the unemployed, a public-works program put many to work.[31]

The Popular Front reform measures had an inflationary effect on the economy, which exacerbated certain economic tensions inherent to it. For example, it was more difficult for smaller businesses to absorb the rising costs of a forty-hour week, annual paid vacations, etc., than for their larger counterparts. Many middle-class Radicals could not but be dissatisfied. In September 1936, the franc was devalued from 6.6 to 4.6 cents per dollar; this temporarily stopped capital from going abroad, but by June 1937 the economic situation had worsened and capital again began to flow abroad in large amounts.[32]

In the middle of June 1937, Blum asked the parliament to grant him plenary powers (to rule by decree) to cope with the exodus of gold and the deteriorating economic situation. Although his proposal received large majorities in the Chamber, the Senate twice turned him down. The conservative Senate was willing to grant plenary power to fight the economic crisis only to one less radical than Blum.[33] A Radical premier then assumed office.

The Popular Front did not last long after Blum's first premiership. Squabbling soon developed between the various groups; their political aims were never similar enough to expect a long-lasting relationship. Also, the clouds of war and consequent rearmament atrophied the desire for social and economic reform and the needed commitment to sustain them. On balance, however, the Popular Front did prove that under certain circumstances, Socialists, Communists, and liberal bourgeois groups could co-operate together and it did foreshadow their future cooperation in France during and after World War II, which led to extensive nationalization and progressive social-welfare legislation.

With the advent of World War II in September 1939, Blum and the Socialists were in the vanguard in defending France against the German Nazi onslaught. The Nazis, however, succeeded by June 1940 in defeating France and occupying three-fifths of it while the remaining two-fifths (Vichy France) became a Fascist puppet state. In September 1940, Blum was imprisoned by the Vichyites, and then tried along with other leftists and liberals in the Riom Trials of February-April 1942. Blum specifically was charged as a former premier and leader of the Popular Front of contributing to the weakening of France by his espousal of extensive social legislation, such as the forty-hour week and annual paid vacations, and for allowing the sit-down strikes in the late spring of 1936, among other things. All of this supposedly led to the defeat of France in 1940. Blum defended himself ably against the various charges, brilliantly proving their ridiculous nature. The trials themselves were peremptorily suspended by the Vichyites in April 1942.[34]

While waiting to be tried at Riom, Blum wrote in 1941 his great theoretical work on socialism. A l'Echelle humaine (For All Mankind), which reaffirmed the basic postulates of socialism.[35] Blum, as his mentor Jaurès did, only partially accepted the economic basis of history (the Marxian view). Co-equal to the material basis is that of the spiritual-moral values developed by mankind over the ages. Blum here invoked Jaurès's concept that "the idea of humanity becomes a principle of progress for civilization in its entirety."[36] (Basically then, the necessary drift toward socialism is viewed by Blum as the realization of humanity's general progress. The similarity of this work with New Conversations of Goethe with Eckermann that he wrote at the turn of the century is remarkable. In both, the Socialist position is given in a largely humanistic way; the appeal being to a higher reason, for moderation in contradistinction to violence as the appropriate means for achieving change.

After the Riom Trials, Blum continued to be held in custody by the Vichyites. Later, he was transferred to the infamous Buchenwald concentration camp in Germany. With the invasion of

Nazi Germany by the Allies in 1945, he was whisked to the Italian Tyrol, where he was liberated by advancing United States forces in early May 1945.

Blum quickly returned to France and plunged into politics. In Paris, on May 20, 1945, he addressed the Conference of Secretaries of Socialist Federations. In *Les devoirs et les tâches du socialisme* (The Duties and Tasks of Socialism), the Socialist position concerning the multifarious problems of life was cogently given.[37] An important point explored was the intimate connection between individual fulfillment and liberty with socialism. In addition, Blum paid tribute to the wartime resistance movement, viewing it as a significant sign of French regeneration.

In June 1945, the French Communist party offered the Socialists a basis for organic unity. In *Le Problème de l'unité* (The Problem of Unity),[38] Blum answered them with what amounted to a categorical refusal. What he did not like about the Communists in France was their tie to the Soviet Union. In particular, he attacked their adherence to the idea that the highest duty of the world's proletariat was to act in defense of the Soviet Union—for Blum the unpardonable sin. This major difference between Socialists and Communists, a fundamental reason for the split at the 1920 Tours Congress, was again the major Socialist objection to unity.

In the Socialist Party Congress of Paris, in September 1946, Blum again talked about major theoretical differences with the Communists and why unity between the two large working-class parties was impossible. For Blum, Socialist participation in government takes place in good faith in contradistinction to the tactics of undermining bourgeois government that is part of the Communist revolutionary conception.[39]

For Blum, democracy always had been a necessary and vital condition for the achievement of socialism. In fact, there is "an indispensable connection between socialism and democracy."[40] Any tendency to acquiesce to class dictatorship which has been noticed in his thought in this period was entirely obliterated. In line with his emphasis on the necessity for democratic development are the ideas laid down in *Notes sur la doctrine,* (Notes on Doctrine),[41] which scrapped the notion of class struggle, prominent in Communist and Socialist ideology, for the concept of action. This view asserts that cooperation between different classes is as equally cogent as the idea of class antagonism. In this connection, Blum reinforces his thesis by intimating that class frictions are certainly not increasing. In the main, it may be asserted that Blum's later thought was not too different from his earlier views of life, that of democratic reformist socialism.[42]

During the years just after World War II, in 1945-1947, Socialists and Communists had great prestige and influence in France. The idealism of the resistance movement against the Nazis during the occupation helped to promote greater solidarity and greatly increased the strength of the French Left. Much nationalization of industry and banking took place through their efforts. About one-fifth of industry was quickly nationalized, as was about two-thirds of the banking capacity, and at least one-half of life and property insurance. In addition, the Socialists were important participants in the passage of extensive social-welfare legislation in such areas as medical care (where most costs are borne by social insurance), wage supplements for children, old-age pensions, unemployment insurance, and four weeks of annual paid vacations. The social security programs in France cover about one-fifth of disposable income.[43] Extensive nationalization and welfare were no mean accomplishments. They allowed for the partial institutionalization of socialism, which for Blum is in the "exercise of power" *("l'exercise du pouvoir")* phase, where Socialist ministries practice the art of the possible, of compromise, of democratic politics. This preparatory phase would ultimately evolve into the "conquest of power" *("la conquete du pouvoir")* phase, or the final realization of socialism.

Léon Blum died in March 1950.

Bibliographical Essay

Blum's more important writings (literary and political works, letters, etc.) are in *L'Oeuvre de Léon Blum* (7 vols.; Paris; Albin Michel, 1954-). All have been published except the one covering the 1914-1934 period. The definitive work on Blum is by Joel Colton, *Léon Blum: Humanist in Politics* (New York: Alfred A Knopf, 1966). Geoffrey Fraser and Thadée Natanson, *Léon Blum: Man and Statesman* (Philadelphia: J. B. Lippincott, 1938), is enjoyable reading, but not overly analytical. It is important because Natanson, a friend of Blum, provides us with many personal details. Richard L. Stokes, *Léon Blum: Poet to Premier* (New York: Coward McCann, 1937), is complimentary with a great deal of information. Colette Audry, *Léon Blum ou la politique du juste* (Paris: René Julliard, 1955), is an excellent work with some criticism. Marc Vichniac, *Léon Blum* (Paris: Ernest Flammarion, 1937), is a fairly good biography, which is almost hagiographic. James Joll, *Intellectuals in Politics: Three Biographical Essays* (Blum, Rathenau, Marinetti) (London: Weidenfeld and Nicolson, 1960), is a brilliant work, mainly sympathetic, but at times also critical. On French Socialism, see Aaron Noland, *The Founding of the French Socialist Party, 1893-1905* (Cambridge: Harvard University Press, 1956); John T. Marcus, *French Socialism in the Crisis Years, 1933-1936: Fascism and the French Left* (New York: Frederick A. Praeger, 1958), and Alexandre Bourson Zévaès, *Histoire du socialisme et du communisme en France de 1871 à 1947* (Paris: France-Empire, 1947). On the differences between Socialists and Communists, see the outstanding work of Annie Kreigel, *Aux Origines du communisme français, 1914-1920* (Paris: Mouton, 1964).

19

Salvador Allende: Chile's Socialist President

by Jack Ray Thomas

Salvador Allende was the first Marxist elected to the presidency of his country in the Western Hemisphere. His particular brand of Marxism, however, differed from the more traditional, doctrinaire type. He believed firmy in Democratic Socialism and he opposed violence, the dictatorship of the proletariat, and, in the formative stages, a monolithic, authoritarian government. Instead, he supported cooperation with existing political parties, input into governmental policies from all political philosophies, and, most surprising of all, close relationships between his government and such traditionally conservative institutions as the church and military.

Salvador Allende Gossens, the martyred president of Chile, was a man who, throughout his political career, made good use of the lessons he learned during a long apprenticeship in government. A medical student during the dictatorship of Carlos Ibáñez del Campo in the late 1920s, Allende became more interested in political solutions to health problems than medical answers. He came to deplore the plight of the poor in his country as they continued to work long and hard for very little reward. When, in 1930, the economic crisis that plagued the world threatened to destroy the Chilean economy, middle-class, professional citizens rebelled and drove Ibáñez to exile in Argentina. Chile's physicians, in particular, were prominent in the anti-Ibáñez movement after police killed a young doctor in a shoot-out with students in Santiago. Allende felt the impact of this event deeply. It was even more a factor in his thinking because he had been reading the works of Marx, Lenin, and Trotsky when the uprising occurred.[1] This experience with the Ibáñez dictatorship led Allende and some of his friends to conclude that the Marxist prediction of capitalism's destruction was accurate, and some of them, Allende included, turned to socialistic political concepts.

In 1933, a number of small, splinter Socialist groups united to form the Partido Socialista de Chile (Socialist Party of Chile). Allende, now firmly committed to a political career, was one of the charter members of the new party. He confined his medical activity to public health from this time on and he sought ways to protect Chile's poor from disease, malnutrition, lack of sanitation, and inadequate medical services. In 1939, a moderate president, Pedro Aguirre Cerda, named Allende to his cabinet as minister of national health. One of Allende's first acts in this important position was to authorize a study of health problems in the nation. The result was a heavily documented, pessimistic look at the health situation in Chile. Allende wanted to publicize the plight of the poor so that public opinion could be enrolled in the fight to improve national health. He believed that once the population became aware of the deplorable situation, dramatic changes would take place. In the report, Allende wrote: "A succinct and cold examination of our medical-social reality is the best guarantee for the diagnosis of the problem and . . . adequate remedies that can reestablish the vigor and health of our peoples can be applied."[2]

Allende's term as minister of public health lasted only a short time because the various parties in the Popular Front government of Pedro Aguirre Cerda began to bicker among themselves and the Socialists withdrew their ministers. The experience, however, was enough to convince Allende that he belonged in politics and, thereafter, he devoted himself completely to a career in government and politics.

During the Socialist party's first decade of existence Allende generally supported his party's leaders in both philosophy and program. This was an age in which welfare-statism and Fabian socialism were more prominent in Chilean socialism than Marxism, and Allende made no effort to shift the thinking of his fellow Socialists to the Marxist philosophy. In truth, the fortunes of the party were so favorable in this nascent period that few members took exception to the position espoused by the leadership. By 1943, however, a small group of Socialists, headed by Allende and Raul Ampuero, concluded that the old-line socialism had served its purpose and that the time had come for a significant change in direction. In that year, Allende ran successfully for the office of secretary-general of the party against the long-term incumbent Marmaduke Grove, thereby increasing the Marxist influence in the party. But the shift to Marxism did not strengthen the party. On the contrary, it weakened socialism because Grove and his followers refused to accept the loss of power and created their own separate Socialist organization which they called the Partido Socialista Auténtico (Authentic Socialist Party). This fragmentation weakened Chilean socialism to the degree that neither of the parties exercised much influence in the immediate post-World War II era.

By 1948, Allende himself was unhappy with his fellow Socialists and he now formed still another splinter party, the Partido Socialista Popular (Popular Socialist Party). Within a few years, however, he recognized the folly of party divisions and led the effort to reunify socialism in 1952. At that time, Allende gained his party's nomination for the presidency of the nation: his first attempt at winning the highest office in the land. He ran again in 1958 and 1964 and, finally, in 1970, on the fourth attempt, he won the presidential office after an extremely difficult campaign.

Throughout the often turbulent history of socialism in Chile, since 1932, Allende was always one of the leading figures. Whether attempting to heal the wounds of interparty strife or splitting the party himself, he was always a major force in the movement. This can be explained partially by the fact that he was one of the youngest of the charter members, and as the older element died off he became a young, elder statesman commanding a high degree of respect from newer members. He was also in the forefront of his party because he was willing to support innovations in theory and he espoused new strategies when old tactics failed to bring the desired end. Moreover, he had wide appeal among the masses. While he was not a great charismatic leader in the mold of his friend Fidel Castro, and while his speeches were usually low-keyed and delivered in a serious and not particularly exciting fashion, there was something appealing about him as a leader, if not his forensic style, then simply his personality. His firm self-assurance and determined attitude exuded confidence. His tenacity won the admiration of the Chilean people, who marveled at his willingness to fight on and on after so often being denied the presidency. In the Latin American sense, he was *macho,* a true man, and this, coupled with his obvious intellectual capacity, made him a favorite of the left-wing element in the country.

As a leader of his party Allende logically became one of its ideologues. To him fell the task of building a Socialist philosophy that would have appeal for a wide range of the Chilean people. Here again, just as his political career was determined largely by events in his country and party, Allende's unique socialism was the product of that pre-World War II age that encompassed dictatorship, depression, and the ascendency of fascism, nazism, socialism, and communism. Prior to World War II, Allende viewed the advantages of cooperation with other left-of-center political parties and groups. He witnessed the phenomenally rapid growth of socialism when coalitions of reform elements even managed to win the presidency. Consequently, it is not surprising that for the remainder of his life he placed great faith in coalition politics.

Allende's determination to cooperate with other political parties was not out of step with the prevailing thought of his countrymen. Chileans historically held a fondness for such politics and Chilean Socialists, as much as any other political group, supported this kind of unified action. As noted, in 1933 the party itself was molded out of a union of six small, splinter Socialist groups. Within six years of the establishment of the party, it had joined in a left-wing coalition to form the Popular Front which elected Pedro Aguirre Cerda president in 1938. While the Socialist leadership soon became disenchanted with the Front, its resolution to bring socialism to Chile in any way possible, including within a coalition, remained strong. In 1957, another coalition was formed which was called Frente Acción Popular (Popular Action Front) (FRAP) and which sought to win the persidency for left-wing parties and for Allende. In 1966 that coalition was dissolved and a new one, called Unidad Popular (Popular Unity) (UP) took its place. It was this group that won the 1970 presidential election for Allende. Consequently, from 1933 to 1970, the Socialist party more often than not was a part of some type of coalition.

Allende's political career spanned that same time period, and his political philosophy accepted the concept of installing socialism in Chile through united action of the left wing. This is not to say that all these coalitions were smoothly operating political machines. On the contrary, each one was characterized by a good deal of bickering and quarreling among the participating parties. One of the continual struggles was a perpetual quarrel between the Communist and Socialist parties. Since both of these elements often claimed the same heritage and since both programs were frequently similar, they naturally sought to strengthen themselves from the same constituency. They competed in the same areas of society for members, and, as political combatants among the working class, they often carried their quarrels into the political coalitions to which they belonged.[3]

One of the primary areas of disagreement centered on the Socialist charge that the Communist party was not a national, patriotic element, but rather a tool of foreign communism that slavishly took orders from Moscow. The two almost split the 1938 Popular Front over the Communist party's adherence to the Russian party line in the early stages of World War II. While Germany and Russia were signatories to a nonaggression pact, the Soviet and Chilean Communist line was pro-Hitler and anti-Allies. But the Chilean Socialist party severely denounced nazism and facism and expressed a willingness to support the Allies in the world struggle.[4] While this issue dissipated when Russia was attacked by Germany and joined the Allied cause, Chilean Socialists could not condone the earlier stance of the Communist party. Additionally, the quick shift in foreign policy also led them to conclude that the Chilean Communists were nothing more than Moscow's lackeys.

Later clashes between the two major left-wing groups touched on the same theme, but both sides managed to keep a reign on their hostility to the other and to cooperate in the face of right-wing opposition. It was in the best interest of each to submerge significant differences. However, the dissension periodically burst forth for the entire nation to witness. For example, in 1962, leaders in each party exchanged open letters expressing their views on the role of the other in the Socialist scheme of things. Raul Ampuero, who had been a close associate with Allende since Salvador became secretary general of the Socialist party in 1943, posited the Socialist point of view which reflected Allende's thinking. Ampuero contended that the core of the difficulty by this time, from which emanated many disagreements, was the divergent concepts of the parties on the issue of violence.[5] The Communists, he charged, were bent on following the Moscow line of establishing socialism throughout the world by the use of force. Chilean Socialists, on the other hand, were pragmatic enough to admit the possibility of bringing socialism to Chile peacefully.

Another area of contention was the old issue of foreign control of Communist party activity. Socialists charged that Moscow continued to dictate policy to Chilean Communists, and, because of this close relationship, Chileans automatically became embroiled in many ideological and practical quarrels that had absolutely nothing to do with Chile. Ampuero admitted that the Soviet Union would always have an important role to play in worldwide socialism, but he argued that Soviet socialism should be followed only as a general guide in social development and not as the absolute authority in all matters.

An additional insight into Allende's attitude toward Communism can be gleaned from a speech by another trusted Allende follower in 1957. Salomon Corbalan insisted that the Socialist party was Marxist, anti-imperialist, and revolutionary. The party accepted dialectical materialism, historical materialism, the theory of surplus value, and the idea of the class struggle. But Corbalan charged that the practical teachings of Marx, Engels, and Lenin should not be viewed as dogma. These men lived and wrote in a different era, in a different region of the world from Chile, and it would be impractical to transfer their thoughts literally from nine-teenth- and early twentieth-century Europe to mid-twentieth-century Chile.[6] The world was vastly different and Chile was not Germany of 1848 or Russia of 1917; therefore, problems in Chile could not necessarily be solved by following solutions expressed earlier and in other nations.

Another facet of Allende's Socialist philosophy was pluralism. He believed that the Socialist revolution could come to Chile while other political parties continued to function and while these parties and their antagonistic leaders retained a measure of power in the government. This idea fit well into his fondness for coalition government, but it went beyond cooperation with left-wing or moderate parties to tolerance of even conservative and reactionary elements. Allende saw this as the essence of democracy. All beliefs and all parties were to be tolerated until finally, on the road to socialism, these reactionaries would be outvoted politically and divested of their power and influence. Consequently, there would be no violent revolution, no excessive bloodletting, and no hostility between the victors and the defeated. Socialism brought about in this fashion was bound to be more painless for non-Socialists and for the nation as a whole; it would be even more beneficial for the Socialists because the bitter struggles that occurred in other revolutions would not be present to destroy cities, farmlands, and populations, and the economy would continue to be healthy, not shattered by warfare. Moreover, this type of revolution would not rip society apart, and it would avoid the sort of lasting antagonisms that would inhibit the policies of the Socialist government and postpone the fruits of socialism far beyond the early months after success.

In his first state of the nation message in 1971, Allende commented on his pluralist government. He acknowledged that this was a new type of revolution, unlike the Russian revolution of 1917, but he did not believe this to be a non-Marxist approach. He said, in fact, that Marxist theoreticians always envisioned such a revolution but expected it to come in Italy or France, where the huge Communist parties were already influential in national politics. No one forecast its coming first in Chile. Thus, said Allende proudly, Chile presented a "second model" for the transition to a Socialist society. This method was ideal for Chile and for the Chilean situation in 1970, but Allende did not advocate it as the only method to be followed by every country. He also acknowledged that some mistakes would be made along the way because the trail that was being blazed was a completely new one. There were no examples to point out errors and to lead Allende and his followers down the correct road to socialism. Chile was, in fact, providing the examples for other countries that might make the effort later.[7]

Earlier, in his inaugural address on November 5, 1970, Allende expressed the same view when he remarked that Chile was fortunate indeed to have avoided a fratricidal war that could have forced upon the nation a long period of costly rebuilding and rehabilitation.[8] But the thought lingered in many minds that perhaps this great Socialist experiment in Chile was not really Marxist! On May 25, 1971, at a press conference for foreign reporters, this question was asked. The questioner wanted to know if perhaps the "second model" that Allende had mentioned earlier was not a heterodox concept. Allende's response was that, not being a Marxist theoretician, he could not comment on the orthodoxy of his system. But he did know that not all countries were alike and that for some, the dictatorship of the proletariat was surely essential but, for Chile, it was not necessary. However, he did concede that his government was for the workers and when he used the term *workers* he meant the proletariat, but still it was not a dictatorship of the proletariat. He concluded that he did not believe such variations on Marxism were dangerous or should be condemned. Finally, he commented that, "If by chance we were to mar the virginity of orthodox theoreticians and yet accomplish something, I would be content with the latter."[9]

One of Allende's reasons for avoiding a violent revolution and espousing a pluralistic system was his abhorrence of violence. In his inaugural address, he pointed out that Chileans all detested domestic clashes and that they were generally a peace-loving people, as proved by their stable past. However, he did not wish to convey the impression that his supporters would not fight if pressed by the opposition. But he hoped to be able to avoid, if at all possible, any physical destruction to life or property while he was president. He believed that Socialists had to continue to demand the rights of the people and that if these could not be secured by negotiation and political means then violence would surely be the result. "Our shield declares it," he said, "by reason or by force. But first comes reason."[10]

This moderate threat to use force remained indicative of Allende's thought on the subject until the last days of his government. He found violence counterproductive, and in his inaugural address he boasted that socialism was coming to Chile without "the tragic experience of a fratricidal war." He then continued proudly, "It is this fact, in all its grandeur, which determines the manner in which this government will set about its task of transformation." Later in the same speech, he noted another good reason for avoiding armed conflict. He said, "Civil war, when imposed as the sole means of emancipation, condemns a people to a rigid political system."[11]

These sentiments remained constant even in the face of growing discontent and increased opposition to his government. In a Labor Day radio and television speech in 1971, Allende reminded his audience that the world was watching Chile and its revolution. He pointed out that when revolutions had been made in other countries the result had been "torrents of blood, imprisonment, and death." Even when these revolutions had been successful the cost had been exorbitant. "It [revolution] has been paid for in lives, comrades, paid for with the priceless lives of children, men, and women." But Allende promised that his revolution was different. "Here we can make a revolution along lines that Chile has established, at the minimum social cost, without sacrificing lives and without disorganizing production."[12]

In another 1971 speech at the University of Valparaiso, he stated clearly his attitude toward revolution in general and toward the Chilean experience. He said:

> I have always maintained that revolution takes place not just at a revolutionary focal point: revolution is not merely an armed section of people in rebellion, nor does it lie only within the electoral field. As a comrade once put it "there are no formulae for revolution." Any one of several methods may be effective, depending on the nature of the country's circumstances.[13]

This attitude comes very close to the view of José Ortega y Gasset, the brilliant Spanish philosopher of the Generation of 1898. Ortega wrote in 1921, "The least important feature of true revolution is violence. It is not inconceivable, though it is hardly likely, that a revolution might run its whole course without a drop of blood being shed. Revolutions are not constituted by barricades, but by states of mind."[14]

At about the same time that Allende was deploring violence to faculty and students at the University of Valparaiso, he was committed enough to this proposition to include it in his first state of the nation address. He reminded his listeners that the Socialist revolution, his revolution, would be accomplished in strictly legitimate terms. He would seek to change those laws that inhibited his movement, but the changes would be brought about in a constitutional manner. Once again he insisted that if counterrevolutionary forces in the nation threatened his revolution, in an illegal attempt to thwart the path to socialism, then violence would of necessity be the result, but he reiterated his pride in Chile for its bloodless revolution and he praised his people for their sophistication, humanity, and discipline in preventing the rise of violence in the nation.[15]

While Allende's abhorrence of violence appears strange for a man bent on revolution, his refusal to condemn totally the work of preceding governments also marks him as a unique revolutionary. His pluralistic system required the assistance of other political parties and other points of view. Consequently, he did not dismiss out of hand the totality of the Christian Democratic program that had been instituted prior to his election. He believed that a basically sound scheme of land reform had already been initiated and that his task was to strengthen and expand it. To his way of thinking, he was merely putting into action that program which former President Eduardo Frei had started. He also pointed out that his program was not something unique but that the plan he set forth already existed in "the minds of a majority of the people of Chile."[16] This being the case, all Allende had to do was to remain within the confines of the legal and judicial system and he could establish his program with a minimum of difficulty.

Democracy for him was a fundamental aspect of politics and he was convinced that democracy could work for him and for the ultimate accomplishment of socialism. In presenting the Popular Unity program Allende said that he wanted to create, "the most democratic government in the history of the country."[17] But, some would ask, Is not socialism in its literal sense an anathema to democracy in its literal interpretation? Does not socialism require a dictatorship of the proletariat as a significant stage on the road to ultimate control? Allende said no to both questions. He argued that socialism could come within a democratic system utilizing existing laws and judicial systems. As noted above, he used Frei's agrarian reform law to distribute land and he invoked an existing law—drafted in 1932—to expropriate foreign-held copper companies. This was accomplished within the strict limits of Chilean law so that it became difficult to convince Allende that he could not carry out the Socialist revolution legally, within the already existent political framework.

In regard to the question of a dictatorship of the proletariat, Allende stated more than once that this was not a necessary stage in the development of Chilean socialism. He agreed that in some countries a dictatorship of the proletariat was essential, but Chile was different. There was no need for socialism to come about in the same way in every country. Chile had simply substituted legalism for this transitional period between bourgeois government and the establishment of socialism.[18] This legalism required cooperation with other political parties, since the Popular Unity did not control a majority of the voters. Left-wing Christian Democrats were important as a force to buttress the Popular Unity, and this meant cooperation. It also meant that even within Popular Unity, some parties were not as radical as others. A United States Socialist, Peter Camejo, complained that the Radical party, which was a member of Popular Unity, had only six years earlier been in a coalition with conservative parties. To be sure, the Radicals were far to the right of the Socialists but their assistance was necessary to strengthen the Socialist cause. Camejo denounced their inclusion in the Popular Unity because he was convinced that Allende had to water down his Socialist views to accommodate them and, in the process, probably alienate the more militant faction of the coalition and even some members of his own party. This situation, according to Camejo, meant that the coalition was not Socialist but instead, a "convergence of opinion."[19] If this was true, then Allende and Popular Unity were not Marxian Socialists, but instead, nothing more than social reformers. Surprisingly, another student of the Chilean revolution, Regis Debray, hinted at a similar view of Allende's philosophy, although he appeared to go along with most of Allende's answers to his questions. Allende's response to all such doubters was that his government was unique and that it was not yet possible to categorize it. Doctrinaire Socialists might object to it but their objections were premature. Allende's belief was that, if it worked, it was right, and he was convinced that he had found the correct route to socialism even if it did not conform to orthodox Marxism.

Another aspect of pluralism was Allende's determination to cooperate not only with other political parties but also with other major forces in the nation. In a March 30, 1971, speech Allende alluded to his government's good relations with the Roman Catholic church. He noted with approval that no great conflicts had arisen between the church and his government. While he represented the masses of the population, the church spoke for a majority of the people. Therefore, it was fortuitous that the two could cooperate so smoothly. He pointed out that the church understood the need for a unified population and was intent on doing its utmost to perpetuate the solidarity that was evident among the Chilean people. He emphasized this point by noting that many religious groups held their bank shares so that the government could assume control over Chilean banking.[20]

This courting of the church was another area in which left-wing opponents criticized Allende's lack of a Marxist perspective. Peter Camejo deplored Allende's inauguration celebration that included a visit to church, where the Archbishop of Santiago greeted him. Allende, however, believed that this was just another normal step along the pluralistic road that he had chosen to pursue. He was determined to cooperate with every organization that had influence in the nation, and the church certainly fit into that category. So long as clerical leaders did not preach a crusade against the Popular Unity government, Allende was willing to do his part to retain cordial relations with even so traditionally hostile an organization as the Catholic church.

Still another example of Allende's tolerance was his attitude toward the military. He was certain that the Chilean officer class was not the stereotypical Latin American autocracy that continually intervened in politics and made civilian political control impossible. He had the lengthy experience of professionalism within the Chilean military to support this view because, after 1932, officers scrupulously refrained from participating in the political wars of the nation. Consequently, Allende hardly could be blamed if he concluded that the professionalism of Chile's military men could be counted upon to keep them from challenging his government. It is not surprising then that throughout his speeches as president, Allende alluded favorably to the military and expressed his confidence in their support for his Popular Unity government.

Skeptics, on the other hand, fretted over the military's lack of commitment to Marxist principles and feared that when Allende got around to invoking Socialist policies necessary for the creation of his ideal state, military leaders would depart from their earlier disinterested stance and confront the government forcibly. In 1971, Allende announced that he was certain that the Chilean armed forces and the national police would "continue to have great respect for the Constitution, for the law, and for the will of the people as expressed through the ballot box."[21] He maintained this attitude well into 1973 when, as the congressional elections of March rolled around and trouble threatened to disrupt the country, Allende brought senior officers into his cabinet as a guarantee to the opposition that the government would not attempt to rig the elections.[22]

When a small group of officers did launch an abortive insurrection in June 1973, Allende again expressed his confidence in the military and this time the barracks revolt was crushed. His cooperation with or, one might say, pampering of the military was more widespread than even his predecessors had dared carry out in less turbulent times. He did everything in his power to please the officer corps. He kept salaries high, furnished modern weapons and permitted officers to continue training with United States advisers. He also sought to give them a new role as participants in developmental projects throughout the nation. At the same time that he was catering to the whims of the military he was careful to prevent the growth of civilian revolutionary militia units that might someday challenge the organized armed forces.

Despite prodding from various segments of his own Socialist party, Allende tried to keep arms away from civilian forces so as not to arouse the ire of the officers. And when his friend, Fidel Castro, sent him a letter in which he suggested that the workers be armed, Allende continued to ignore this advice, believing that he could resolve his political difficulties without arming civilians and thereby encouraging a civil war between leftists and the armed forces. [23] Uppermost in Allende's mind was his determination to avoid bloodshed at all costs. Yet, after the abortive barracks revolt of June 1973, he apparently began to change his attitude, and arms flowed into the country destined for civilian hands. In the three months between the first uprising and the final military overthrow of the government, Allende obviously wavered in his policy of keeping arms from his civilian supporters. The military government's white paper, published after Allende's fall, documents the storing of arms and the initiation of guerrilla training sites throughout the country. It also charged that Allende's presidential home on Tomás Mora Street in Santiago contained a large cache of arms. Still, Allende kept a tight reign on his more violence-prone associates until the military uprising actually began. There is little doubt from his speeches and from his actions prior to September 1973 that Allende wanted to cooperate with the military, to avoid arming a paramilitary group, and to prevent extensive bloodletting in his country.

Allende's determination to bring about socialism in a peaceful and legal manner led one observer to comment that he was "a good man." The same writer believed that he was also an idealist who wanted to wipe away the misery, poverty and backwardness of his country in a quick and painless way. But, in trying to achieve these laudatory goals, he made two mistakes. First, he tried to establish socialism peacefully with too thin a power base. He was elected to the presidency with only 36 percent of the vote and even the subsequent congressional elections gave Popular Unity only 44 percent in the 1973 parliamentary elections. With less than half the people in support of his program, it was inevitable that the courts and congress would challenge his policies and that without a sharper mandate he could not, in a peaceful way, bring about the kind of Socialist system he wanted. The second mistake was his handling of the economy. The nation was solidly behind his nationalization of foreign copper companies, but when he later moved against domestic business interests he did not receive firm popular support. Then, as the economy slumped after the expropriation of the copper companies, even some workers turned against him. Copper miners struck for higher wages, a phenomenon which Allende could barely comprehend since the nation and the workers now owned the mines and therefore they were, in Allende's eyes, striking against themselves. But it was the bourgeoisie that felt most threatened, and it was the bourgeois truckers who, by striking, precipitated the economic collapse that led to the military intervention and Allende's eventual overthrow.[24]

Doctrinaire Marxist writers, however, were predicting failure for Allende's government months before it fell, because it did not follow the Socialist blueprint for success. Allende continued to abide by the Constitution and sought to balance the bourgeoisie against the proletariat. He needed both sides in developing his program, and he never realized that he could satisfy neither by trying to appeal to both. He nationalized some industries but he never seemed to understand that nationalization, of and by itself, could not eliminate capitalism. Of the more than thirty-thousand businesses in Chile, less than 1 percent were scheduled for purchase or nationalization. Therefore, it was obvious that capitalism was bound to continue in the nation despite Allende's protestations that he was creating a Socialist state.[25]

While critics from both the right and left assailed Allende, a more balanced approach indicates that he did have some accomplishments to his credit in his short-lived term of office. His nationalization of foreign-held copper mines was supported by the overwhelming majority of the Chilean people, and, even with a pro-United States military government now in power, no one has suggested that the copper companies be returned to their previous owners.

Allende also increased wages to the proletariat by an average of 35 percent and, although this contributed to the astronomical inflation that struck the country during his regime, the salary increase was long overdue. The president also set in motion agricultural reform that reduced the number of large landowners and created a significant number of landholding farmers. He could not gain passage of new legislation to accomplish this objective, but he could and did use existing laws.[26]

Unfortunately, others in his government were not as patient as Allende, and violence flared as peasants attempted to forcefully take the lands from their legal owners. Allende tried to bridle such impatience and to take the cases to court so that every step in agrarian reform would be in keeping with the legal processes of the nation. Left-wing critics condemned his legalism and badgered him to move more rapidly. Moreover, moderate and right-wing opponents charged that he was remiss in not preventing the takeover of land and the bloodshed that periodically developed. Allende was caught between both sides and could please neither one. Certainly, little that he did could be regarded as valuable by the moderates and conservatives. They opposed him on philosophical grounds, and even measures that might be beneficial for the nation were rejected out of hand, sometimes only because their author was a Socialist or, more often, because he was publicly labeled a Communist which stirred up even greater passions among the opposition.

But left-wing criticism of Allende at times was also unreasonable. One United States Socialist chided him for not supporting Bolivia's demand for an outlet over Chilean territory to the Pacific Ocean.[27] No Chilean president, from whatever party, could suggest the return of territory won on the battlefield during the War of the Pacific, 1879-1883. This would have been political disaster for Allende or any other elected official. It might appear to be a logical course of action for a Marxist to put into motion a maneuver that would fit into Marxian internationalism, but Chile is a nation in which nationalism is exceedingly powerful, and even Socalists and Communists could not find a majority of their members to support such a suggestion.

A less outlandish criticism, but nevertheless one that Allende could not effectively silence, was that he should have aided North Vietnam in the struggle against the United States. Not only did he not send aid to the Vietnamese, but he never officially condemned the United States intervention. Here again, international

realities of the instant did not permit such a policy. Allende
wanted to retain a working relationship with the United States.
Economically, he needed credits and loans that the United States,
if angered, could block. Therefore, he concluded that he was not
in a position to assist any other nation; Chile was experiencing
her own severe economic problems. Allende's condemnation of
the United States also would not have been materially beneficial
for North Vietnam and would certainly have worsened United
States-Chilean relations. Therefore, practical political considera-
tions prevented him from following policies that some Marxists
believed necessary.

Allende could not bring socialism to Chile overnight as many
hoped and expected. No true social revolution is ever accomplished quickly, and the peaceful model that Allende was attempting requires even more time than one that relies on destruction
and rebuilding. Therefore, it was unrealistic to assume that even
in a full six-year term of office Allende could have accomplished
all that he had set out to do. Certainly in a limited three-year
term, he could achieve even less. This having been said, however,
it must also be pointed out that Allende made mistakes as president. But in his defense how could it have been otherwise? For
twenty years, he had played the role of opposition, and then for
three years he was responsible for the decisions that had to be
made. Such a transition from loyal opponent to government in
power is not effected overnight without some serious errors taking
place along the way. Then too, as noted earlier, Allende chose
to operate within a coalition government, and such a system
naturally placed many obstacles in the path of the executive as
he tried to satisfy a number of different constituencies. Finally,
even before he became president, the opposition rewrote some of
the constitutional provisions, strengthening the legislative branch
of government at the expense of the executive. Allende had to
accept this change as a condition for the presidency because he
was a minority president and the presidency was in the hands of
the Chilean congress which had an opposition majority.

With all of the problems confronting him, with a chaotic
political situation to step into, and with only a little more than a
third of the population solidly behind him, it is remarkable that

Allende was able to accomplish as much as he did. Some of his achievements must be attributed to the man himself, to his personality, perseverence, and grasp of reality. He was committed to a dream, but he tried to realize the dream by employing realistic, sane, peaceful policies. Even then, the forces arrayed against him were unstoppable. Allende tried desperately to bring socialism to Chile peacefully, but he failed. Nevertheless, he devoted his life to improving the lot of Chile's poor. No better epitaph can be written for any man.

Bibliography

Allende, Salvador. *La realidad médico-social Chilena*. Santiago: n.p., 1939.

Allende, Salvador. *Nuestro camino al socialismo*. Buenos Aires: Ediciones Papiro, 1971.

Allende, Salvador. *Primer mensaje del presidente Allende ante el congreso pleno, 21 de Mayo 1971*. Santiago: Talleres Gráficos Servicio de Prisones, 1971.

Allende, Salvador. *Chile's Road to Socialism*. Baltimore: Penguin Books, 1973.

Camejo, Peter. *Allende's Chile: Is It Going Socialist?* New York: Pathfinder Press, 1971.

Castro, Fidel, and Beatriz Allende. *Homenaje a Salvador Allende*. Habana, Cuba: Editorial Galerna, 1973.

Corbalan Gonzalez, Salomon. *Partido Socialista*. Concepción: La Academia de las Escuelas de Ciencias, Polticas y Administrativas de las Universidades de Chile y de Concepción, 1957.

Debray, Regis. *The Chilean Revolution: Conversations with Allende*. New York: Vintage Books, 1971.

Drake, Paul W. "The Chilean Socialist Party and Coalition Politics, 1932-1946," *Hispanic American Historical Review* 53, no. 4 (November 1973):619-43.

Feinberg, Richard E. *The Triumph of Allende: Chile's Legal Revolution*. New York: New American Library, 1972.

Chapter 2

Anarchism

Jean Grave and French Anarchism

by Louis Patsouras

Jean Grave, along with Peter Kropotkin, was a foremost exponent of anarcho-communism—the leading Anarchist current in contemporary history and which may be taken to represent the term "Anarchist"—in the late nineteenth and early twentieth centuries. In contradistinction to its main opponents in the broad stream of socialism: democratic socialism and Soviet communism, anarchism, ever revolutionary, opposed the gradualism of the former and rejected the authoritarianism of the latter because it seemed to have contempt for individual civil liberties. For Anarchists, socialism and liberty are synonymous. To this end, they were ever aware of the dangers posed by the bureaucratic state (whether Capitalist or Socialist) and its analogous counterpart in technological development, the large corporation. The aim of the Anarchists was and is a humanization of life in which liberty and harmony are paramount.

Jean Grave (1854-1939) is one of the more significant figures of nineteenth- and twentieth-century anarchism in particular and socialism in general. For many young Anarchist militants in the generation before World War I in Europe, Grave personified the active and committed Anarchist who maintained a sustained revolutionary tension between himself and bourgeois society. In André Malraux's *Les Conquérants* (The Conquerors), Rebecci, an Italian Anarchist who ended up in Canton, China, as a proprietor of a store specializing in shoddy European goods, recalled his youth in which Grave's influence was paramount: "Jean Grave was not just a good man, he was my youth. . . ."[1]

41

When we look at the life and ideas of Grave, we must
first mention that he is one of the few Socialist thinkers and activists of prominence to come from a working-class background:
his father was a shoemaker.[2] (Most of the Socialist leaders were
middle class and turned to socialism primarily for intellectual and
moral reasons.) As a youth in Paris, Grave went through the fire
of proletarian existence. Like most children of the proletariat he
had scant schooling—about five years. At the age of eleven he
went to work, joining his father, mother, and slightly older sister.
In order to survive, the average working-class family had to have
all of its members working from an early age. Despite various
hardships, Grave was reasonably happy and secure in the family.
Concerning his early life and interaction with his parents, Grave
informs us that he had an authoritarian father who blamed his
son for his own faulty work (he worked with his shoemaker
father for some time), and a gentle mother who tried to protect
him from an abusive father.[3] The relative security of his early
life was shattered in Grave's late teens when his beloved mother
and sister died in quick succession. His father passed away while
Grave was in his early twenties.[4]

One may ask what sustained this young worker in the face
of social misery and the personal despair of losing his family?
The ray of light that allowed him to overcome it all was a hope
for a Socialist world, where mankind would live in equality, freedom, and brotherhood. Already as a teen-ager, he had experienced the revolutionary euphoria of the Paris Commune of 1871,
the most significant uprising of the European Left in the nineteenth century.[5] Its aims were to continue the struggle against
the German invaders and to usher in a Socialist republic. The
Commune, which lasted only two months, was enthusiastically
supported by the young Grave; he was proud of his father, who
enrolled in its National Guard. For Grave, the ideals of the
Commune were the hallmarks of his anarcho-communism. They
included the ownership and management of production by all the
people; the popular election of officials, who would receive average wages and be subject to immediate recall; and the destruction of clerical influence and superstition.[6]

In 1874, Grave was drafted by the military and became a
marine. The young Grave brilliantly and sensitively informs us of

what it was to serve in the military. In his autobiography, *La Grand Famille* (The Big Family), a novel of severe realism, we see the brutality of military life, which Grave tells us was based on the principle that the inferior in rank must obey the superior.[7] Not surprisingly under these conditions, we see a milieu where fear and tension are firmly ensconced. In the military, where the aim is to dehumanize man in order to allow for the formation of a robot-killer,[8] the lowly soldier can take out his frustration and anger only sexually—either on the personification of degradation in bourgeois society, the hapless prostitute, or by raping the women of "inferior" conquered groups.[9] Grave understood well the innate horror of a class society, which the military reflects to a greater than average degree, one based on authority.[10]

After an early discharge from the military as the only surviving member of the family able to take care of his ailing father, Grave soon plunged into Socialist activity in Paris. In early 1880, Grave was instrumental in founding the Social Study Group of the Fifth and Thirteenth Wards of Paris. This was the first bona fide Anarchist group there since the catastrophe suffered by the Paris Commune.

Although Grave had only five years of formal education, he taught himself the art of writing by being incessantly involved with it as secretary of the Fifth and Thirteenth Sections Anarchist Group in Paris. He became the editor of *Le Révolté* (The Rebel) in 1883, which was published first in Geneva, Switzerland, then transferred to Paris in 1885. In 1887, *Le Révolté* became *La Révolte* (The Revolt). In 1894 it was closed by government repression against Anarchist journals and newspapers due to Anarchist propaganda by deed (violent acts committed against the government—such as throwing bombs in the Chamber of Deputies and at homes of government prosecutors).

When government repression was lifted in 1895, *The Revolt* became *Les Temps Nouveaux* (The New Times). Under Grave's able direction it became one of the great newspapers of Socialism in the twentieth century. It lasted to the outbreak of World War I, when the government shut it down as part of its crackdown on "dangerous" Socialist groups.

What makes *The New Times* so unique is not only the intellectual brilliance of its staff, but also, under Grave's prodding, its interest in both politics and art. On politics, there were penetrating articles on Anarchist theory and activity, in addition to articles on international working-class developments by many outstanding intellectuals: Grave himself; Elisée Reclus, a leading geographer and noted Anarcho-Communist theoretician in his own right; Peter Kropotkin, an Anarcho-Communist with a worldwide reputation as a naturalist and one of the giants in the Socialist spectrum; and Fernand Pelloutier, an Anarcho-Communist who is known as one of the fathers of the French union movement and founder of revolutionary syndicalism. All wrote for The New Times.[11]

With reference to art, we shall first mention the *Literary Supplement* of *The New Times* in which social criticism imbedded in the works of great writers was reprinted; Leo Tolstoy and Emile Zola were among the more important here. In the visual arts, outstanding neo-impressionist painters who were Anarcho-Communist—for example Paul Signac and Camille Pissarro—and the world-renowned lithographer and socialist, Alexander Steinlen, contributed to the paper. Their lithographs depicted the cruelties and social misery inherent in bourgeois civilization, while at the same time showing the heroism and dignity of the proletariat in the face of adversity.[12]

Grave was an outstanding pioneer in the Socialist spectrum who fused art to socialism; this should not be surprising, especially if we take into account that he was, in his own right, an outstanding writer. He was well aware of the importance of art in fostering a Socialist conscience and world view. Grave's own artistic endeavors in literature are considerable. In addition to *The Big Family,* he has two other novels to his credit—*Terre Libre* (Freeland) and *Malfaiteurs!* (Evildoers!)—and a play titled *Responsabilités!* (Responsibilities!).

Freeland, published in 1908, is a tightly written, action-packed, utopian-revolutionary work. It's about a group of revolutionaries exiled to a remote Pacific island who successfully revolt against their guards and then set up an island utopia based on Anarcho-Communist principles. One of the highlights in the novel is when the guards try a counterrevolution, but are thwarted because the new system is not coercive—physically lazy people not forced to work discover the counterrevolutionary plot in time.

In *Evildoers!*, Grave deftly examines the problem of social mobility as opposed to revolutionary commitment. Two young friends, both proletarian and revolutionary, take different paths in life. One becomes successful, a Socialist deputy in the Chamber of Deputies, well on his way to making money; the other, a dedicated Anarchist militant, refuses to compromise his ideals and, Prometheaslike, endures prison and other privations. They are married to sisters. For the opportunist, the marriage is a hollow shell as he has the usual mistresses; for the dedicated revolutionary, the marriage is successful, as there is love. Grave's contention is that socially mobile opportunists use people, including their mates, and, as such, must pay the price of psychological loneliness; their predatory inclinations are sensed by others, who then feel distant toward them. In a world of strife based on individual and social antagonism, those who succumb to its ethic become morally and socially warped to one degree or another—they are alienated.

Grave's only play is *Responsibilities!* This excellent work is based on the model of a Greek tragedy, where there is a moral conflict between two values, both seemingly of great merit, with one, however, having precedence over the other. An Anarchist militant converts a friend to anarchism. The friend loses his job and is imprisoned for Anarchist activity. His wife, from the tension engendered, kills their two children and herself. The Anarchist who converted his friend is grief-striken by this tragic chain of events. He asks himself whether, indeed, it would not have been better to have let his friend alone and thus have prevented the death of three innocent people. Another friend (fate), however, consoles him, stating that the just struggle for anarchism must go on despite the loss of innocent lives.[13]

Let us come now to the problem of anarchism's relative decline in France and other industrialized nations, which started with the outbreak of World War I. Although anarchism was traditionally antiwar, Grave and Kropotkin supported France and her allies against Germany during World War I, reasoning that a

French defeat would unleash the German Kaiser's despotism throughout Europe and thus strengthen reactionary forces.[14] The antiwar Anarchists, of whom Errico Malatesta was the most well known, continued the traditional antiwar pattern in denouncing all wars, which they charged arose from the authority of the state, capitalism, and other forces.[15]

In November 1917, the successful Communist revolution in Russia burst over the world horizon. Within a brief period of time, it divided the international Socialist movement into two basic groups—those who supported the revolutionary Communists and those in opposition, who were largely reformist Socialists. Grave and Kropotkin from the beginning opposed the Communists, while many other Anarchists were friendly to them.

The divisions caused by World War I and the Communist revolution decimated French anarchism. Many left the movement out of disillusionment or joined other left-wing movements. From 1921 to 1936, Grave edited a magazine which appeared infrequently, *Les Publications de "La Révolte" et "Temps Nouveaux"* (The Publications of "The Revolt" and "New Times"). Its circulation was only in the hundreds. Grave and others tried in vain to revive anarchism in France. Anarchism as a movement was dead but its ideas continued to germinate and are important in contemporary life.[16]

In the nineteenth century, those who preached the "religion" of inequality—the nobility and the bourgeoisie—had already a serious rival in socialism; socialism developed in the milieu of the Industrial Revolution, which created a new class in history, the working class or proletariat, which lived in the new and vast cities of the brave new world of industrialism. There are many reasons why socialism was able, from a historical perspective, to quickly challenge capitalism. To begin with, the age of industry brought about mass literacy, which allowed for some worker politicization, and democratic forces already in motion were able to better consolidate their position. Until the 1848 revolution, socialism was basically of the utopian variety, which postulated cooperation between the proletariat and the bourgeoisie. Afterward, however, as socio-economic tension within capitalist society increased, socialism generally became militant and developed a philosophy which was clearly antithetical to capitalism. The three main streams of socialism in the twentieth century—communism, social democracy, and anarchism—by evolutionary or revolutionary means postulate the termination of capitalism by the creation of a Socialist society.

Anarchism, which means absence of government, is indeed a significant part of socialism. Although its roots go far back in history, it was only in the eighteenth-century French Enlightenment that it had some impress in philosophy and literature. Denis Diderot, one of the great philosophers of the eighteenth-century Enlightenment, for example, in his *Supplement to Bougainville's "Voyage"* postulated a society that contained many Anarchist elements. By the beginning of the nineteenth century, some of the great minds were already Anarchist. William Godwin, an outstanding British intellectual of this period, a friend of Samuel Coleridge and father-in-law of anarchism's greatest poet, Percy Bysshe Shelley, in his *Enquiry on Political Justice* cogently developed the principles of anarchism. Significantly for Godwin, man by reason (the importance of a humanist education was stressed) would inexorably be led to realize the benefits of a society where cooperation would replace the wasteful features of a society dominated by private property and social class.

The father of modern anarchism, however, is considered to be Pierre Joseph Proudhon, the great rival of Marx in nineteenth-century socialism. Basically, Proudhon's basic ideas are under the rubric of mutualism. It foresaw a peaceful transition from capitalism to socialism, where a central bank would provide interest-free loans to worker cooperatives, which in time would supplant capitalist enterprises. The cooperatives themselves would be run by the workers. Proudhon, himself from a working-class background, who worked in industry for many years and who was always intimately associated with workers, was more than confident in the ability of the working class to do this. In mutualism, small private property is also allowed. Concerning the problem of coordinating various public functions, the decision-making process would be in small political units, the communes, which would be federated nationally and internationally. Basically, Proudhon's anarchism reflected a condition in which small industry and agriculture were still dominant.

The revolutionary element in anarchism after the mid-nine-teenth century was led by Michael Bakunin, a Russian nobleman who was the romantic revolutionary par excellence of his time. Ever willing to sacrifice his life for revolution and always setting up clandestine revolutionary groups—even as figments of his fertile imagination—this great hulk of a man spread anarchism via his disciples in Italy and Spain. The revolutionary collectivism of Bakunin saw a working-class revolution which would replace the bourgeoisie with a system of collectivistic associations of work-ers and farmers—no private property would exist. The groups would be run by the people and Bakunin envisaged a system con-cerning public decisions similar to Proudhon's.

In the late 1870s, a new form of anarchism came about: anarcho-communism. Basically, it differed from past forms of anarchism in that attention was focused on need and not work-time to compensate the producers—as was the case for Proudhon and Bakunin. In other words, the associations of production and distribution did not operate on a salary system! Producers would work in harmony and deposit goods in warehouses where, in turn, as consumers they would take what they wished! Private property would not exist even as a concept. The local commune would be the unit where a sense of fraternity would prevail in the various endeavors of life. The local communes would be feder-ated nationally and internationally and would send representatives for periodic conferences. The greatest exponents of these ideas were the former Russian prince, Peter Kropotkin, and his chief disciple, Jean Grave.

Underlying the ethic of anarcho-communism is mutual aid. A key work of Kropotkin, *Mutual Aid: A Factor in Evolution,* is central to understanding this concept. According to Kropotkin, even though in the evolutionary process there is the normal antag-onism between species, within each one the dominent factor is mutual aid or cooperation based on a deep-seated sociability that developed in order for the group to survive successfully. Grave, in his famous *La Société mourante et l'anarchie* (The Dying So-ciety and Anarchism), talks about the importance of solidarity in society, a term which is similar to that of mutual aid. On bal-ance, this view sees that the individual and social antagonisms of contemporary class-ridden society are not representative of man's basic humanity. Over a period of time, mutual aid, fostered by such working-class institutions as unions and activity for revolution, will bring about a society where the exploitation of man by man will forever be abolished. The Anarcho-Communists in their stress on man's sociability are in the Rousseauist tradition. (Jean Jacques Rousseau, the greatest social philosopher of the eighteenth-century Enlightenment, maintained that individual man was corrupted by institutions first engendered by private property —class society, war, etc.)[17]

In their criticism of bourgeois society, Grave and the Anar-cho-Communists are at least the equals of the Marxists. Grave unsparingly criticized all bourgeois institutions and, indeed, saw that they were leading mankind toward the abyss of social ca-tastrophe. The underpinning of this was a social structure of a bourgeois world, which condemned most people not only to a life of relative poverty, but also to one of indignity.

The inner social tensions which reflected a basically preda-tory society—one based on power—could not but spill into inter-national relations. By the first part of the twentieth century, the advanced capitalist nations—Great Britain, France, and Germany, for example—were imperialistic rivals. According to Grave, co-lonialism or imperialism was tied to general economic tendencies within capitalism which forced it to seek new areas to exploit economically for raw materials and for new markets. He saw an ever-increasing armaments race, also intimately tied to im-perialism, which itself was a cause for war.

Tied to the rise of imperialism and increasing social tensions, there arose a jingoistic nationalism which stressed the "unique-ness" of the nation in respect to others. Just as there were different social classes based on relative superiority, so there were the "unique" characteristics of ethnic groups which would allow the "better"' groups to dominate the "inferior" ones. In this world of Social Darwinism, Grave was aware of one of its major com-ponents, racism. Racism is a cultural attitude affecting not only the bourgeoisie and nobility but also large sections of the prole-tariat of advanced industrialized bourgeois nations, who scape-goated to compensate for their own economic and social inferi-

ority. Grave saw that a predatory civilization could not but view
the colonialized peoples that it had conquered as inferior and
therefore to be exploited at will. In the world of class tension,
of aggressive nationalism that was tied to rival imperialisms, of
racism, of an ever-increasing armaments race, Grave correctly
foresaw the inevitable holocaust that was to be known as World
War I.[18]

Grave's intense criticism of bourgeois society is coupled to the
problem of how to change it for a new society. Grave at first
(to about 1900) generally believed that society would be changed
in a series of revolutionary happenings. In a romantic revolutionary mood, he saw the imminent destruction of bourgeois
society as coming through the efforts of a few dedicated revolutionaries who would commit propaganda by deed in order to
awaken the lethargic and intimidated workers to begin revolution
for socialism. In this connection, Anarchists during this period
were against the idea of voting for representatives to political
assemblies. Voting was seen as a sham in a world of great socioeconomic inequality: the monied interests had an insuperable
advantage in influencing the outcome of elections through bribery
and other means.

After this romantic revolutionary phase, Grave shifted his
revolutionary focus to where proletarian institutions would take
a more active role. Unionism now became an important factor in
the equation for revolution. Grave was somewhat suspicious of
workers' unionism, since much of it was reformist and practical
in nature, and as such generally accepted capitalism. He foresaw
that a revolutionary overturn could come from a series of strikes
progressing to a general one, which would paralyze society and
allow the workers and other progressive groups to bring about
socialism. Interestingly enough, Grave here sees that the revolution would not be made only by proletarian groups, but also by
others. Presumably much of the peasantry and even sections of the
lower-middle class would be involved in the change. Involved here
were the majority of the people.

By the beginning of the twentieth century, Grave saw that
a revolutionary overturn of bourgeoisie society would not come
quickly, but take many generations. This not only recognized the

tremendous socioeconomic dominance of the bourgeoisie, but also took into account that their value system was accepted by most people. As such, he saw that the people were not sufficiently politicized to accept socialism in one fell swoop, but that they were interested in specific social reforms that directly affected their lives. Grave foresaw a long gestation period where piecemeal reform would come about by voting, which he now at least partially accepted and which he saw as a concession to the people extracted from the ruling capitalist groups. The general tenor in this line of thinking is that revolution in France and other advanced capitalist nations will come not from groups that are brutally exploited and dehumanized, but from those that enjoy a rising standard of life and which from the vantage point of greater human dignity and politicization will demand and participate in change. At a certain critical point, the popular forces would achieve an overwhelming numerical majority and opt for a Socialist society. Obviously, economic downturns, which capitalism could never entirely cure, would play an important role in the scenario for ultimate changeover. Since the bourgeoisie would not wish to relinquish acquired socioeconomic privileges, fighting probably would erupt. Upon its completion, the state itself, with its various arms—bureaucracy, police, army, courts, etc.—would be swept away and all productive private property would be expropriated. It seems as if the social revolution would not only be national (for example, France) but would soon become international. It must be added that Grave and others are vague in this area.[19]

It is only after the revolution that serious disagreements exist between Anarchists and other Socialist groups (basically the Marxists). Both the Marxists and Anarchists saw that the end of socialism was anarchism—the abolition of the state. They differed, however, in the pace toward achieving it. Involved with the timing were such various key concepts as manual versus intellectual labor, the level of the productive forces, and the possibility of a bourgeois counterrevolution.

Marxists saw the state as withering away gradually under Socialist direction: it would still be needed for a rather long period of time, perhaps generations, in order that its centralized power forestall any possible bourgeois counterrevolution, and be-cause the state itself would exist until various social antagonisms under socialism would be resolved. The antagonism inherent be-tween intellectual and manual labor was a key social contradiction to be resolved before a stateless society. For the Marxists, the existing large plants and extensive division of labor with its hierarchy of managers and workers would have to continue for a long period of time. Concretely, the intellectual workers would receive higher wages (wage labor would exist for the Marxists until the advent of anarchism) and thus in the beginning phase of socialism (the one before anarchism) there would yet remain the individual and social antagonism inherent in this structure of wages and work. Social antagonisms would ultimately be abol-ished as the productive capacity of industry would increase and the cultural institutions of socialism would allow all to enjoy a high economic standards of life and high cultural level to bring about integrated labor, the synthesis of intellectual and manual labor.[20]

The Anarchists were categorically against this Marxian theo-retical pattern. They believed that modern technology (using electric energy, for example) could be used effectively to decen-tralize the forces of production in order for the quick elimination of large-scale industry with its hierarchy and division of labor. This in itself would greatly aid the rapid realization of integrated labor. In addition, the immense cultural resources of the people would be quickly set in motion in order to quickly erase technico-cultural differences. As for waiting until the supposedly higher productive level to occur in the future would make everybody unselfish, the Anarchists stressed that the forces of mutual aid would be sufficiently strong after a successful Socialist revolution to overcome this particular problem. In this respect, the Anarchist pattern of historical development puts more attention in purposeful human volition and ethical behavior than does the Marxian one, which would stress level of productive forces. In other words, the Anarchists are more optimistic than the Marxists as to how quickly Socialist man will emerge. Concerning the problem of possible bourgeois counterrevolution, the solution of Grave was that of the armed people. As such, a centralized state army was not necessary.

For Grave, the two-phased Marxian syndrome to achieve full socialism was fraught with great danger. He and other Anarchists were afraid that the bureaucrats and intellectual workers—who would still represent authority—might try to preserve and indeed even reinforce the differences between them and the people. Instead of bureaucracy and continuing socioeconomic inequality, Anarchists from the beginning would have a system of integrated labor, devoid of salary distinctions, where participatory democracy in all avenues of life would reign. All would work and participate in management in essentially small productive units. Obviously Anarchists are not so naive as to reject all large-scale industry. Steel, for example, was seen as being a large-scale situation. However, the thrust toward smallness and integrated labor would not allow the exceptions to generally alter the basic framework of the new society.

The basic aim of anarchism is to realize unalienated man (where socioeconomic tensions leading to aggression and loneliness, for example, do not exist any longer). The individual is linked to the general community by a sense of freedom and work creativity, which at the same time not only increases individuality, but which strengthens mutual aid. Economic selfishness as we know it today would, under the conditions enumerated, be rather unusual.

Let us now look more closely at how Anarchist society would be run by participatory democracy. This has to do with the political in a general sense of the term. The nucleus here is the local commune, organized from a relatively compact geographical area and with few people. It would hold periodic meetings, where all community matters would be discussed. Committees would be formed to further explore particular economic projects that would affect the total community—the building of a railroad line, for example. Disagreements, of course, could arise. Such disagreements would be decided by majority vote within the commune. The new society would not eliminate disagreements; it must not be forgotten, however, that underlying antagonisms of class do not exist here. As such, the vote of the majority can not be basically coercive in a society where mutual aid permeates general activity. On a national level, there would be a federation of communes, and internationally, a federation of nations. Obviously there

would be a great network of more-or-less permanent committees
to coordinate relations. In a society of cultural-technical equals,
without a wage system, where rotation would be practiced in
various committee assignments, and where the individual is not
confronted by class distinctions, it would be difficult for a bureaucratic group to arise that would be more equal than others.[21]

After the successful revolution of the Russian Communists
under Lenin in November 1917 and the inauguration of a Communist government, there has been much controversy within the
Socialist spectrum concerning its virtues and faults. Grave and
other Anarchists were among the more trenchant critics of communism as practiced in Russia, which they basically saw as a
deformed form of socialism. To begin with, Grave was against the
dictatorship of a party which did not even have the backing of
the majority of the people. In these circumstances, Grave sus-
pected that those in power had to rely on fear and repression,
not hallmarks of socialism as conceived by its notable thinkers.
In this connection, the elimination of anarchism by the Communists, as indeed of all opposition within the Socialist spectrum,
could not but bring about ill-feeling. Also, the destruction of civil
liberties, freedom of speech and press, for example, by the Communists was unthinkable under traditional socialism. For Grave,
Russian communism was a system of state capitalism, which
greatly exploited the working class as the trade unions in Russia
were not autonomous organizations, but under bureaucratic government control. Not surprisingly, Grave saw that in Communist
Russia the state bureaucracy, which included such parasitical elements as the army and secret police, had to subsist on the backs
of the proletariat. In fact, the growth of this bureaucracy was
directly related to the unpopularity of communism. In order to
impose their rule, the Communists under these circumstances had
to strengthen their positions by enlarging the bureaucracy, a class
whose interests would be antithetical to those of the proletariat.
The yardstick for Grave concerning how good a society basically
is has to do with authority, which may be seen by the amount of
social inequality and coercion in any society. Obviously Communist Russia for Grave could not be a good society, run as it
was as a dictatorship by a new ruling class of bureaucrats. The
dictatorship of bureaucrats imposed on the masses was itself hier-

archized and undemocratic. These two features produced power struggles by various factions that were resolved by periodic purges —often horribly bloody—where hundreds of thousands of Communist party members were literally murdered by the secret police. The winner in the various power struggles was a paranoid madman feared by all, a new tsar—Stalin. It must be pointed out here that despite serious theoretical disagreements between Anarchists and Social Democrats over the future of Socialist society, they both decried the loss of civil liberties and other non-Socialist features of Communist Russia.[22]

Although Anarchists were a numerically minuscule group, certainly under five thousand in France in the first quarter of the twentieth century, anarchism has had great impact on the French labor movement and in the world of art. Even though anarchism had a period of decline as a result of World War I and the Russian Communist revolution of 1917, it is now enjoying a renaissance in France and other nations, including the United States.

Anarchist influence on French labor is via anarcho-syndicalism and revolutionary syndicalism. (The nuances from an overall historical view between these two movements are small and we may consider them together under the latter appellation.) In the early decades of the twentieth century, the most powerful and militant union in contemporary France, the National Confederation of Labor (La Confédération General du Travail) (CGT) was largely run by Revolutionary Syndicalists.

Many of the leading Revolutionary Syndicalists had been Anarcho-Communists. Indeed, the father of revolutionary syndicalism, Fernand Pelloutier, one of the giants of the French labor movement, always saw himself as an Anarcho-Communist. Paul Delesalle, an assistant secretary of the CGT, was a prominent Anarcho-Communist before joining revolutionary syndicalism. Basically, it wasn't too difficult to make the transition from anarcho-communism to revolutionary syndicalism since the latter is simply workers' anarchism. Its stress is on union organization, which would be the nucleus: (1) for educating workers both technically and culturally; (2) for conducting the class struggle against the employer class until the final victory of the proletariat —revolution—would come through a series of strikes culminating in a general strike; and (3) for the organization of future society. After the revolution, the respective unions would not only run the factories, but also the various community services. Participatory democracy, the abolition of the wage system, and integrated labor are the hallmarks of revolutionary syndicalism.[23] Grave feared that the formality of union organization might develop a group of bureaucrats, but apart from this the closeness of basic ideology shared by the two groups is undeniable.[24]

Grave, despite the reservation noted, cooperated with revolutionary syndicalism for a primordial reason—the revolutionary union movement would play the leading role in the coming social struggles and ultimate revolution. Pelloutier and Delesalle reported extensively on the labor movement in *The New Times*. Grave knew both well. Delesalle, in fact, was among his closest friends.[25]

The impact of the Enlightenment in which relativism and reason were significant components, the French revolutionary tradition, and the slow industrialization that allowed for the continuance of small enterprise and localism, among other elements, all contributed to the importance of anarchism in France, which in the generation before World War I played an important role in the cultural picture.[26] Léon Blum, an outstanding literary critic and the first Socialist premier of France in 1936-1937 stated near the turn of the last century that everyone more or less was interested in anarchism. The leading literary journals of this period— *La Revue Blanche* (White Revue) and *La Plume* (The Pen) were unabashedly Anarchist. Grave's synthesis of art and politics in *The New Times* was a reflection of this cultural pattern.[27]

A sizable portion of Anarcho-Communist philosophy is very puissant in the contemporary politico-cultural stream: the New Left, which dominates the student movement in France and other nations, with its emphasis on participatory democracy in all avenues of life, is a strong echo. In the spring of 1968 it triggered in France a spontaneous social revolution in the form of a general strike of over ten million workers (manual and intellectual), which lasted for many weeks. Although the general strike failed to topple President Charles de Gaulle, his prestige was so seriously eroded that he resigned some months later. Among the strikers, the ideas of erecting a Socialist society based on participatory democracy and integrated labor were prevalent.[28]

Bibliographical Essay

The great work on French anarchism is by Jean Maitron, *Histoire du mouvement anarchiste en France, 1880-1914* (Paris: Société Universitaire, d'Éditions et de Librarie, 1955). On a general history of anarchism, see the outstanding work by George Woodcock, *Anarchism: A History of Libertarian Ideas and Movements* (Cleveland: Meridian Books, 1962). Other useful works include: James Joll, *The Anarchists* (New York: Universal Library, 1966); Gerald Runkle, *Anarchism: Old and New* (New York: Delacorte Press, 1972); and Murray Bookchin, *Post-Scarcity Anarchism* (Berkeley: Ramparts Press, 1970). On Jean Grave, see Louis Patsouras, *Jean Grave and French Anarchism* (Dubuque, Iowa: Kendall/Hunt, 1978).

Chapter 3

Communism

Georgi Dimitrov and the United, Popular, and National Fronts

by Clement Masloff

The Bulgarian Communist Georgi Dimitrov became in the 1930s the personification of anti-Fascist Popular Fronts throughout the world. But long before the Leipzig trial and his subsequent elevation to a top position in the Comintern, his formative years as a Bulgarian labor leader had shaped his flexible, pragmatic political methods. Dimitrov exemplified the plodding, practical, nondogmatic Marxist leader and strategist with roots in trade unions and industrial struggle. He won final victory by transcending theory.

In the 1930s, Bulgarian Georgi Dimitrov became the international symbol of anti-Fascist fronts of Communists with Social Democrats and left-wing groups throughout the world. The leader and main voice of the revolutionary Third International, with its center in Moscow, he exemplified tactical flexibility. His task under Stalin was to find anti-Fascist allies. Dimitrov bestrode the political stage of this Popular Front era prior to World War II as a star hero, after being catapulted to fame by the historic Leipzig trial. There he had turned the tables on the Nazi prosecutors trying him on trumped-up charges of having planned the burning of the Reichstag building in Berlin. Only when we examine his early career in his native Bulgaria can we discover the forces that made him the right man to symbolize the enormous political turn toward alliances and flexibility that international communism took in the years of the Hitlerite threat to both the East and the West.

Born into a poor refugee family from Turkish-ruled Macedonia, Dimitrov's youth was vastly different from that of most of the intellectuals who founded Bulgarian socialism after studying in England, Switzerland, and Russia. His father, a carter, was eking out a living in a village near Radomir, along the western Bulgarian border, when Georgi was born in 1882. Dimitrov was schooled in the hard daily life of the Bulgarian worker, which he lived and shared. He alone among the Socialist pioneers in Bulgaria rose from the trade union movement rather than the teaching intelligentsia. His father took his wife and four children to the capital, Sofia, in order to learn the hatter's trade from a brother-in-law who in the process also converted him to Protestantism. His mother sent her children to an American missionary school in 1892 and dreamed that her bright Georgi would become a minister of this minute sect in Orthodox Bulgaria. His expulsion from the school after two years, for reasons never clarified by historians, threw him onto the crowded Sofia labor market at the age of twelve or thirteen. He ran away from apprenticeships with a carpenter and a blacksmith, only finding his calling when a neighbor invited him to learn the printer's trade. The grass-roots radicalism of workers' clubs and the printers' union became the incubator of his socialism and career as a labor leader. Literate, radicalized printers were his comrades and teachers. Soon he was writing satires of his former missionary teachers, printing anonymous pamphlets against them on the sly.[1]

Dimitrov's rise to labor leadership was swift. In 1900, the year he read the *Communist Manifesto* and became a Marxist at the age of eighteen, he followed an elder brother into the secretaryship of Sofia printers' organization. He continued to work as a compositor until 1905, despite his rising position. He joined the Social Democratic party in 1902, immediately prior to its historic division into a reformist faction of the Broads and a more doctrinaire group of Narrows. In fact, Dimitrov found himself at the fulcrum of this split into two rival Socialist parties.[2]

The rigidity of the Marxism of Dimitar Blagoev, called the "grandfather of Bulgarian socialism," led to struggles and divisions as soon as a party was organized in 1891. In 1892, a Social Democratic League broke away from Blagoev's narrow doctrinaire ideology, but was reunited in 1894. As a student in Russia in the 1880s, Blagoev had taken part in the earliest of purely

Marxist groups. Georgi Plekhanov, who had to break away from and struggle against Russia's populist socialism in order to establish a Marxist ideology suitable to that backward empire, was the primary intellectual influence upon Blagoev, and therefore the Narrows, throughout his life. Since Bulgaria was not yet in a stage of industrial capitalism when the party was formed in 1891, Blagoev had to devise a general, speculative projection of where Bulgaria was headed. He followed Plekhanov in thinking that Bulgaria, like Russia, would follow the same path of economic development and final revolution that Marx had devised for the industrial West. Rejection of native populism and disdain for the peasantry became part of the legacy that the "grandfather" left to the Narrows tradition.[3]

Factional fights broke out at party congresses in 1901 and 1902. The character of the party and its relationship to the peasant and the artisan were the main topics of conflict. Yanko Sakazov, the leader of the Broads, attacked Blagoev's dogmatism by calling for an alliance with all "productive strata," such as small tradesmen and peasants, in order to insure "social progress" and democracy. Actual division into opposing factions began in the Socialist fraction in the National Assembly. Peasant votes had been crucial in winning six parliamentary seats in 1899. Some deputies tried to cooperate with liberal reformists, claiming they were responsible to their peasant electors, even if this meant disagreeing with the rigid prohibition of political alliance required by the Central Committee.[4]

In February 1903, Dimitrov was elected secretary of a group of fifty Narrows who broke away from the Broad majority dominating the party unit in Sofia. Disagreeing with an organizational report, Dimitrov led a walkout and formed an autonomous committee. Three of the five members of the Central Committee, led by Blagoev, recognized this splinter as the official organization, precipitating an avalanche of separations nationwide. Dimitrov had arrived on the political stage as a splitter and divider. A party Congress in July expelled the Broads, revised the organizational constitution, and set the ideological foundations for a new Narrows party.[5]

The division was parallel to, but not identical with, the division in Russia between Bolsheviks and Mensheviks later that same year. The Narrows differed considerably from Lenin's new party; the peasants of Bulgaria were not viewed as potential allies of the proletariat, but as a dangerous majority that might infiltrate and water down the party's ideology. The attempt of the Broads to collaborate with reformers was castigated as opportunistic compromise with the petit bourgeoisie, while their stress on purely economic goals for the trade unions was likened to Eduard Bernstein's revisionism in Germany. Blagoev came closest to Lenin in his acceptance of the idea of the party as the directing vanguard of the proletariat. The Broads accused him of sectarian splitting and intellectual elitism. Both groups exaggerated their differences once the division began. The Narrows became polarized as extreme leftists, totally antipeasant in ideological orientation.[6]

Dimitrov became a typical Narrows doctrinaire, seeing both the Broads Socialists and the rising Agrarian Union as mortal foes. As a traveling strike organizer setting up unions under exclusively Narrows' control, he developed into a shrewd tactician and infighter. Turning up wherever the Broads' unions called economic strikes, he often succeeded in taking them over, adding revolutionary political propaganda to primarily labor disputes. In 1909, he entered the Central Committee of the Narrows party, also becoming secretary and chief of the labor federation built upon Blagoev's political principles. He opposed efforts by the Broads to unite separated unions of typographers, dock workers, carpenters, iron workers, miners, and many other trades into general, nonpolitical unions. Opposing unplanned, spontaneous walkouts, Dimitrov preached the need for iron discipline, order, and strong leadership in labor struggles. He would only accept merger with Broads' unions on his own terms: the expulsion of moderate reformists from any new united labor movement. Only revolutionary Marxism could provide a basis for true solidarity and cooperation, he believed. Dimitrov came to dominate the Narrows' Labor Council, a combination of the party's Central Committee and the secretariat of its labor federation. He spoke for the unions within the Central Committee, and for the political leadership within the tightly organized unions.[7]

Dealing with day-to-day labor struggles, Dimitrov had to operate with more tactical flexibility than the strictly political leaders, mostly intellectuals, of the Narrows. In specific strikes, circumstances at times forced him to cooperate temporarily with his ideological rivals among the Broads. He grew sensitive to how changing conditions might necessitate tactical unity in a crisis, to be followed by a return to mutual rivalry and conflict. In 1912, Dimitrov was sentenced to a month in the Sofia prison on the charge of having called a Broads union leader a police spy.[8]

Dimitrov's maneuverability was confined to strikes. The doctrines of the Narrows held that the party and the unions were two forms of the identical organized social democracy of Bulgaria. In 1905, a faction of "anarcho-liberals" who became a Proletarian League were expelled from the Narrows, while in 1908 a Progressist group was thrown out. In both cases, the issue was the dissidents' desire for immediate reunion of the two Socialist parties and their rival labor federations. Party discipline was tightened; anyone advocating compromise with the Broads was treated as one of the Broads. Leon Trotsky tried to mediate between the two parties in 1910, but soon fell into bitter polemics with Blagoev, accusing him of splintering and forming an isolated, militant, political sect unwilling to make any compromises toward reunion. Although in April 1914 a conference over unification was held between the two competing labor federations, it failed over the issue of the Broads' nonpolitical, strictly economic view of trade unionism. Dimitrov even quarreled with German labor chiefs, such as Karl Legien, who had come to conciliate them.[9]

Elected to both the National Assembly and the Sofia City Council in 1914, Dimitrov became immersed in social and labor legislation, continuing as the head of the Narrows' labor federation. In a short time, he emerged as party spokesman on housing, social insurance, sanitation, and municipal problems. During World War I, he focused upon practical issues of labor conditions, food supplies, and war refugees. He failed to win squatters' rights in Sofia on vacant land. But, in 1919, he led in the successful fight for the eight-hour day in the National Assembly. The very nature of his labor and legislative assignments made him the most practical-minded Narrows leader. Working in a context of multi-party and multi-union competition for mass support, he acquired a sense of political timing. Dimitrov was prepared to cooperate with rivals on proximate gains if he thought this would bring a proletarian revolution closer.[10]

Practicality in politics did not soften his Marxist fervency. In 1918, he was arrested for having emotionally told a wounded soldier to disobey an officer's order to vacate a train compartment for him. While in prison for having incited such "mutiny," the hot-tempered Dimitrov quarreled with Agrarian leaders also sentenced for antiwar activities. He showed contempt for even their leader, Aleksander Stamboliskii, as "the representative of the petty bourgeoisie".[11]

In later years Dimitrov was to regret his negative reaction to the Radomir uprising of September 1918. Crowds of disaffected soldiers and peasants marched on Sofia. At the time, he saw it as a reactionary revolt of village against city. Even though its main force came from the unpopularity of the war, it nearly toppled the government. The Agrarian leader Stamboliskii seized the initiative and joined this spontaneous march upon Sofia, hoping it could create a republic. This peasant-soldier crowd of ten to fifteen thousand was dispersed after one battle on the outskirts of the capital, the Narrows staying neutral during the crisis. Proposals for a worker-peasant alliance from Stamboliskii were refused by Blagoev. The latter profoundly distrusted the peasantry and feared that unacceptable concessions would have to be made to the rural majority in order to form a coalition. The new regime of Lenin in Moscow severely criticized this dogmatic refusal to support a peasant republic in 1918. At the time, Dimitrov shared this anti-Agrarian bias, seeing the Radomir revolt as a quarrel within the bourgeoisie, between its urban and rural elements.[12]

Blagoev castigated Stamboliskii for becoming prime minister under Tsar Boris in October 1919. Increasingly, the Narrows saw the Agrarians as their main enemy and obstacle. Expecting world revolution at any time, the new BKP (Bulgarian Communist party) saw no profit in joining any coalition government under Stamboliskii, who seemed suspiciously ambivalent toward the BKP. Would he try to exploit and betray them? Stamboliskii trusted the artisan class more than the urban proletariat as an ally of the peasantry. His attacks on lawyers, bureaucrats, and the intellectuals smacked of utopianism. Most of the BKP, including Dimitrov, saw him as a Kerensky who would disappear once a truly revolutionary situation arose. This moment seemed to have arrived in December-January 1919-1920, when a railroad strike nearly became a general political strike. Stamboliskii was merciless in suppressing what nearly grew into a coup. Dimitrov, the commander of the strike, went into hiding, being saved from arrest through the intervention of his wife with the Agrarian leader Kosta Todorov. The attempted general strike was called off as a fiasco.[13]

For the next three years both the BKP and Stamboliskii underestimated the potential danger from the Right, so intently were they watching each other. Each viewed the other as its main problem, thinking that if its rival were eliminated, it would have a clear road for the rebuilding of Bulgarian society. The BKP overestimated the strength of the Agrarian regime after its failure with the strike in 1920. Made confident by electoral gains, the Communists planned to win the villages from the Agrarians. The military coup overthrowing Stamboliskii on June 9, 1923, found the gravely ill Blagoev advising Communist neutrality. Dimitrov was one of the three party officials responsible for the decision to take no action. The coup was seen as "a fight of cliques of the rural and urban bourgeoisie for power." Dimitrov and his colleagues refused to intervene in what looked like a struggle between forces equally anti-Communist. Revolutionary rhetoric served as an excuse for inaction. The decisive moment was allowed to pass. The BKP now entered a period of deep trauma.[14]

The Bolshevik revolution had had the full support of Blagoev and his party, which had been a founding member of Lenin's new Third International (the Communist International, or Comintern) in March 1919. Although the Narrows renamed their party to signify their adherence to the new international revolutionary movement, Blagoev was slow and hesitant in applying Leninist concepts and tactics to the internal situation within Bulgaria. The Narrows tradition of inflexibility was too congealed. The BKP ignored Comintern policy set in 1922 urging peasant-worker regimes wherever possible. Blagoev believed it was impossible to have any alliance with Bulgarian Agrarians, whatever the international situation elsewhere might be. His hope was to drive the Agrarians out of the villages by converting and recruiting peasant activists and building a "united front from below." Only a few days after the overthrow of Stamboliskii, Dimitrov stated at a union meeting that workers throughout Bulgaria had been and still were indifferent to the rightist coup, that nothing could have been done anyhow. But soon the new regime of Aleksandar Tsankov began a brutal terror campaign against not only Agrarians, but the BKP too. The Comintern sent angry messages to the Central Committee, criticizing its continued passivity and defeatism. Vasil Kolarov returned from Moscow and joined the top party leadership; soon a new course was set. The old tactic of competing in the villages against the Agrarians was dropped. Approaches were made to the radical wing of the Agrarians. Underground arming for insurrection began as the party came to realize the extent of its misjudgments.[15]

In a series of articles starting as early as May 1, 1923, before the coup, Dimitrov had launched a campaign for a united labor front with the Socialists, the old reformist faction of the Broads.[16] Yet he continued attacking the Agrarians, accusing them of secret agreements with the Western capitalist powers.[17] His tactic for gaining a united front with the Socialist unions included public attacks upon their leaders as allies of the bourgeoisie and appeals to their followers to merge with the Communist unions, a united front from below.[18] But, on May 1, he recognized for the first time that there were two proletarian parties in Bulgaria. He called for a common political front, not just trade union cooperation. It was rejected by the Socialists, just as his proposals for union merger on his terms had been for many years.[19]

For the next twenty years the failure to cooperate with the Agrarians to avert the debacle of June 9 was the center of factional dispute in the BKP. A second trauma was the poorly planned BKP uprising against the military regime in September 1923. Although the Communists negotiated with the left wing of the Agrarians in the days immediately prior to the futile uprising, each party acted independently. Hundreds of BKP members were already under arrest. After a week of unsuccessful guerrilla fighting in rural areas, the insurgent bands retreated into the mountains in defeat. Dimitrov and the other revolutionary commanders fled into Yugoslavia from a new White terror of repression and execution.[20]

Dimitrov was not to return to Bulgaria for twenty-two years. His career became international. From Yugoslavia, Dimitrov defended the rationale behind the September revolt. He opposed the growing acts of individual violence by bands left in the mountains, calling for a united front with the Agrarians against the rightist regime. He proceeded to Vienna, helping form an Exile Committee to act for the shattered Central Committee. As editor of an exile newspaper in the Austrian capital, he had to set type himself at times. Dimitrov organized Bulgarian students into an anti-Fascist coalition led by Communist youth. Through the Exile Committee, he linked the Central Committee being restored within Bulgaria to the Comintern in Moscow. Dimitrov defended the September rising from exile critics who called it inappropriate and adventuristic.[21]

In January 1924, Dimitrov presented Communist proposals to the Agrarian Kosta Todorov for a combined revolt to overthrow the Tsankov regime. A worker-peasant government was to follow, with six Agrarian ministers and four Communists in the cabinet. Dimitrov demanded the premier be a Communist. The key ministries of war, interior (with the police), and communications were to fall to the BKP. He promised the Agrarians Russian arms and a training base near Odessa if they would co-opt Communist members onto their revolutionary committee preparing for insurrection. These talks were moved from Prague to Moscow, where Dimitrov turned down the Agrarian proposal for a joint revolutionary committee with an equal number of Communists and Agrarians, and plans for a future peasant government with no seats for the BKP. No deal could be reached. Dimitrov's parting shot was an angry outburst that he would find other allies.[22]

Dimitrov's moves toward the Agrarians were always reluctant and distrustful, the result of desperation and necessity. His natural bent was toward a labor united front with the Socialist unions. He saw the disciples of Stamboliskii as adventurers chasing a political mirage. Their concept of a purely peasant regime, with proletarian support, could become a danger to the BKP should the latter ever stand in its way.[23] Labor, not peasant politics, was his forte. In January 1924, he proposed that a new Workers' party be organized by the remnants of the BKP in Bulgaria. The former was to operate legally, while the latter went underground to direct its actions. Dimitrov thus took the initiative away from the party right wing seeking the end of illegal activities. Only selected activists were to continue in the BKP, while the new party would keep contact with the masses and deal with daily, practical labor issues. Although soon banned, this Workers' party conceived by Dimitrov set the pattern for the flexible dualism of organization in the 1930s. Dimitrov succeeded in preventing the breaking away of the right wing into its own new legal, mass party, while drawing new members into the broadly based legal front.[24]

Dimitrov now condemned the passivity of June 9 and affirmed the correctness of the September rising. But he was gradually falling out of step with the party leaders in Bulgaria, who were turning leftward. A secret conference on Mount Vitosha near Sofia in May 1925 elected him to the Central Committee and approved the policy that led to the September rising, but was silent about the growing spontaneous counterterror by the remaining left-wing armed bands. In a letter of February 17, 1925, Dimitrov with foresight warned Kolarov of the risks to the party in independent resort to violence. He got the Exile Committee to call for the end of preparations for armed insurrection and to focus upon the immediate needs of labor. The BKP failed to head his warnings in time to avoid catastrophe. An April 16, party leftists independently attempted a bombing in the Sofia cathedral while Tsar Boris was attending a funeral. This unsuccessful adventure in would-be assassination proved Dimitrov right about the danger of not having liquidated the half-disciplined guerrilla groups still at large. An unprecedented wave of repression and executions fell upon BKP now, with more casualties than even in the September rising of 1923.[25]

As the regime exploited the explosion in mounting an anti-Communist terror campaign, the party organization in Bulgaria crumbled. By 1925, Dimitrov, Kolarov, and their centrist followers had defeated the party right wing that wished to end all illegal activities. The bombing and its aftermath ended the previous uneasy cooperation between Dimitrov's group and the insurrectionary left wing. A crisis of morale rose in the BKP. A forty-day conference in Moscow, from July to September 1925, called by the Exile Committee, signaled a victory for the position of Dimitrov and Kolarov. The doctrinaire attitude inherited from the Narrows against political flexibility and alliances was amended. "Revolutionary compromises" similar to those of Lenin were to be accepted, as long as they did not fall into "opportunism." The Comintern policy toward peasants was to apply to Bulgaria despite past differences with the Agrarians. The new slogan was to be a worker-peasant government to restore democracy through a united front with the Agrarians. The overthrow of the Right's dictatorship was a goal that could attract the rural masses not ready or eager for revolutionary Soviet-type power yet. After any popular uprising the BKP and the Agrarians would necessarily have to share power. The two parties would remain autonomous, with separate ideologies, while operating in a common front. Criticism of Agrarian leaders would have to continue in order to keep the revolution on track. At this conference Dimitrov for the first time began to outline the organic bond between the struggle for popular democracy and future Socialist revolution that was to later become his most famous ideological theme. A worker-peasant state which would end dictatorship from the Right and limit the power of the bourgeoisie was a giant step toward proletarian victory.[26]

This historic conference offered full support to the Left Agrarians in their goal of trying to draw the bulk of the peasants to their side. This would weaken the Agrarian Right and Center, who refused to ally themselves with the BKP like the Left. Appeals for unity were directed at professional associations, cooperatives, political groups of independent self-employed craftsmen and artisans, and refugees from Macedonia, Thrace, and Dobrudzha. Because of the near collapse of local Agrarian organization in 1923, no attempt would be made to draw remaining village members into the BKP. The conference authorized aid to the Left Agrarians in reviving their structure and press. Support was even voiced for a purely Agrarian regime, if that alone could end the Right's dictatorship. Dimitrov expressed concern that the party had needlessly attacked potential allies in the past, failing to exploit the divisions among the various strata in the bourgeoisie.[27]

Accepting the fact that capitalism had been stabilized in Bul-

garia, Dimitrov attacked those still supporting immediate insurrection. He admitted his own responsibility in the debacle of June 9,
but went on to criticize the ultra-Left, led by Peter Iskrov. After
the conference, Dimitrov stayed in Moscow as the BKP representative with the Comintern. He now spent most of his time on Comintern assignments: uniting the Bulgarian exiles, blocking both
right and left deviations in the BKP. In early 1926, he led an
attack upon the German ultra-leftists such as Ruth Fischer. Put
in charge of the regional Comintern secretariat for Poland and the
Baltic states, Dimitrov came to feel he was not devoting enough
time to his own Bulgarian party.[28]

In the late 1920s Dimitrov worked on international tactics of
united labor fronts from below, through winning workers away
from reformist leaders. Although he urged joint strikes and demands, common congresses, and calm polemics with Social Democratic rivals, he insisted upon refusal of any political compromise
with moderate Socialists anywhere. Bulgarian Communist labor
leaders were advised to relentlessly unmask reformists before their
followers.[29]

At a BKP Central Committee meeting in Vienna in September 1926, the left faction of Iskrov mercilessly castigated the "wav-
ering center" of Dimitrov and Kolarov. Iskrov's faction attempted
to take control of the party with the slogan "more weight to the
young." Although the older leadership temporarily blocked this
radical surge for power, Dimitrov's confession of tactical errors
with respect to the June 1923 debacle forebode coming
difficulties.[30]

A new leftward turn by the Sixth Comintern Congress in
August 1928 destroyed the power of the Vienna Exile Committee
and centrists such as Dimitrov within the BKP. The students and
exiles led by Iskrov used insurrectionist rhetoric to castigate all
those with a pre-1923 history in the Narrows party. In the summer
of 1929, these leftists won a majority at a Central Committee
meeting held in Berlin. The Comintern did not oppose this takeover. Bad days came for Dimitrov in 1930 when the Iskrov group
took control of the Bulgarian department of the Comintern. Their
demand that he not work in Moscow led to a hunt for a suitable
distant post. The League Against Imperialism, located in Berlin,

appeared a good sinecure. With Iskrov in firm control of the BKP, few would have given Dimitrov much chance of ever influencing Bulgarian events again, or of ever rising from his long fall.[31]

During his political eclipse from 1928 to 1933, Dimitrov had few articles published in the press of the Comintern or the national parties. Also, during this period, the Iskrov group attacked him repeatedly for the June 1923 events and other "mistakes": he had lowered his sights to a worker-peasant regime rather than striving for a Soviet government, had allied the party with petty bourgeois Left Agrarians, and had truckled to "social Fascists" in his attempts at trade union unity and merger—despite the fact that it was within a Marxian political framework.[32]

In August 1932, Dimitrov attended an international antiwar congress in Amsterdam that featured celebrities such as Maxim Gorki, Upton Sinclair, Albert Einstein, and Theodore Dreiser. Organized by the French Communist writers Romain Rolland and Henri Barbusse, and financed by the master-builder of popular mass organizations in Germany, Willi Munzenburg, it was attended by 2,195 delegates from around the world, only 830 of whom were Communists. Dimitrov who made not one public speech at the affair, directed and coordinated the activities of those connected with Comintern parties. He was aiming at the legalization of his league's activities in all European countries. As formal head of the Comintern's Western European section, such trivial publicity-making tasks had become his main occupation. Only his arrest by the newly formed government of Hitler at a Berlin restaurant on March 9, 1933, saved him from obscurity, hurling him onto history's center stage. The subsequent year-long trial in Leipzig, his bold defense against the false charges of having planned the burning of the German Reichstag, and his courtroom attacks upon fascism made him an authentic hero of the 1930s, a worldwide rallying point for antifascism.[33]

At this, the zenith of his life, he fulfilled to the hilt the part presented him by fate. From the bottom of his political career, he instantly became a world figure, the focus of resistance to Hitler. Dimitrov prepared for the confrontation with his accusers, attending the prison chapel and getting into long debates with a Catholic priest on the comparative merits of Protestantism and Catholicism, thus sharpening his command of German for his trial. In court, Dimitrov took over his own defense, exposed the methods of Hitler's brand of justice, questioned witnesses and made objections, and was ejected from the room five times. From a victim, he turned into the moral prosecutor of fascism.[34]

After his release and air flight to Moscow in February 1934, the now famous Bulgarian became an intimate of Stalin, head of the Comintern, and one of the primary spokesmen for world communism.[35] In the spring of 1934, plans for a Comintern Congress in June were dropped. Already Dimitrov had written a speech draft proposing that Communist parties everywhere drop tactics permitting only united fronts organized from below. Had the Congress been held that year, he would have called for dealing directly with Social Democratic leaders to construct united political fronts from above. The slur term "social Fascist" would have been forbidden in criticism of Socialist reformers. The Peruvian Communist, Eudocia Ravines, has recalled that while in Moscow in the spring of 1934, he asked Dimitrov what he thought of the scheme of the French writers Henri Barbusse and Romain Rolland for a broad movement of anti-Fascist, antiwar forces across all of Europe, open to Communists, Socialists, laborites, liberals, Catholics, and democratic groups in general. Dimitrov indirectly revealed that it was perhaps Stalin who was preventing greater Comintern tactical flexibility, answering: "That project of Barbusse and Rolland? I am heartily in favor of it, but there is little sympathy for it. . . ."[36]

Dimitrov, always a cautious political operator, was never one to get out too far ahead of others. His acute sense of timing was his stength. In 1933 and 1934, Stalin and the Comintern saw the only solution to the problem of anti-Communist fascism in the formula of immediate world proletarian revolution. Not until the Seventh Comintern Congress in August 1935 did Dimitrov have the opportunity publicly to unveil the tactic of the Popular Front. In his speeches as head of the Comintern, he presented to this Congress a new way of dealing with the Fascist menace: victory over it *within* the framework of the capitalist system. Recognizing a difference in nature and quality between parliamentary democracy and Fascist dictatorship, although both rested upon a capitalist economic base, he held that the defeat of the Right would not necessitate a total political and social revolution, but only a cleaning out of the superstructure above the productive base. Democratic liberties and free elections were a benefit to the workers that had to be protected. The final uprooting of capitalism remained a task for the future. Nazism was the immediate problem. Dimitrov proclaimed, "We Communists have other aims than the defense of democracy . . . but in struggling for our aims we are ready to fight jointly for any immediate tasks which, where realized, will weaken the position of fascism and strengthen the position of the proletariat."[37]

Dimitrov set only one condition for the formation of Popular Fronts; the new allies must be genuinely against war and fascism. In this, they would be aiding the Comintern and fighting fascism's capitalist offensive against Communist movements. Marxists should criticize and attack only those bourgeois forces that blocked or hindered formation of a common, Communist-led, anti-Fascist front. Communist parties could even go so far as to participate in Popular Front governments with anti-Fascist programs in those cases where this was popular with the masses, who might be willing to battle fascism, but were not ready yet for a proletarian revolution. Such a government might go as far as to take control of industrial production, disband the old police, establish a workers' militia, and provide full opportunities for Communist party activities. Dimitrov thought France the best chance between democracy and fascism, not between capitalism and a Socialist revolution. Dimitrov accused the ultra-Left in many parties of having long underestimated the capitalist Right, while also overestimating the degree of working-class disillusion with Social Democratic reformism and politically neutral labor leaders. Dimitrov foresaw capitalists and the parties of the upper bourgeoisie in more and more countries abandoning parliamentary democracy and allying with fascism. Increasingly, Social Democrats would be forced to seek Communist support to counter the rightward trend of the bourgeoisie. A Popular Front with Socialists did not entail accepting their reformism. He believed that the skilled workers of the world, the backbone of reformist unions, were already taking more radical positions because of the danger of fascism hanging over them. Communists were to ally themselves only with those Socialists who accepted a Popular Front program. Such an alliance could only strengthen the revolutionary potential of all workers by moving everyone in the coalition closer to Communist positions[38]

A Popular Front was an alliance from the top down. It would in no way hamper independent Communist initiatives. It could be broadened to include peasants, the urban petty bourgeoisie, students and intellectuals. Its foundation was political cooperation between party leaders. At the 1935 Congress Dimitrov used the terms "united front" and "popular front" as equivalents, making no important distinction between them. He set three conditions to forming a Popular Front government: (1) the existing regime would have to be so weak that the bourgeoisie could not prevent a Popular Front government by force; (2) the masses opposed fascism but were not ready for Soviet power; (3) most of the members of the other parties in the Popular Front were demanding the suppression of fascism to such a degree that they were cooperating with the Communist party against the anti-Communist factions in their own organizations. Only the fulfillment of these demanding conditions could justify a true Popular Front government. The Popular Front coalition in France was far from this stage yet. Such a regime would clearly signify that conditions would soon be ripe for a proletarian revolution.[39]

Communists could enter Popular Front ministries even before the onset of this prerevolutionary crisis, in order to prepare for it. Communist power would come about through this preparatory stage of Popular Front government, not outside or against it. This phase was not meant to destroy capitalism, only to liberate it from fascism in such a way as to bring about the conditions for a proletarian revolution. Such a "democracy of a new type," halfway between bourgeois democracy and Soviet power, did not mean any peaceful, gradual evolution toward socialism, said Dimitrov. At no time during this congress did he ever rule out eventual violence. The most that might develop on its own from a Popular Front government was a vaguely defined "democratic dictatorship of the working class and the peasants." But he saw no way to escape the inevitable revolution that had to come before a truly proletarian state existed.[40]

Most of the delegates who heard Dimitrov were unable to use his Popular Front tactics at home. Probably it was Tito, present at this congress, who most successfully followed the road to power mapped out by Dimitrov in 1935. In World War II, Yugoslav Communists mobilized a Popular Front movement, army, and government with the support of peasants and student radicals. The Yugoslav anti-Fascist movement did not interfere with the organizing of a future Communist regime. Tito kept his ultimate revolutionary goals in temporary abeyance, preserving a "government in readiness" within his broad anti-Fascist front. He carried Dimitrov's tactic into areas unforeseen by its author.[41]

Dimitrov's Comintern power led to the rebirth of his influence within the BKP. In March 1935 the Bulgarian exiles met in Moscow and adopted the Popular Front tactic. Most of the ultra-Left was purged and executed in Stalin's capital. Even then opposition to the new course continued within Bulgaria. The Comintern rebuilt the old Workers' party, but now in the underground. This new organization attracted the old centrists, willing to follow Dimitrov into a Popular Front. A confusing dualism prevailed, with the leftists in control of the BKP, while the pro-Dimitrov forces had a different name and structure. Not until 1940 was the left wing completely rooted out, when the Workers' party absorbed what was left of the BKP.[42]

Victory for Dimitrov's tactic in Bulgaria came with World War II and his announcement of an invitation to a Fatherland Front in July 1942. By then a Russian citizen and a deputy to the Supreme Soviet, Dimitrov's main job was running the Comintern bureaucracy. Vasil Kolarov led the day-to-day activities of the BKP through the war. Dimitrov did not manage to return to Burgaria until November 6, 1945, over a year after a Fatherland Front government had followed Russian occupation in September 1944. This ill and exhausted national hero became head of the party and the government.[43]

At the Fifth Congress of the BKP in 1948, Dimitrov, as general secretary, defined the stage of people's democracy Bulgaria was then in as an alternative to the Soviet form of proletarian dictatorship. Bulgaria had already moved beyond the kind of Popular Front government described by Dimitrov in 1935.

If the Fatherland Front of World War II had been a more national version of an anti-Fascist Popular Front, then people's democracy signaled the start of the construction of a socialist economy, under a proletarian dictatorship unlike the Russian version, which resulted from a classical revolution as evisioned by Marx.[44]

The BKP's allies in the Fatherland Front were split, tamed, purged, and eventually fully controlled. The smaller radical groups even merged directly into a broad Fatherland Front organization. Dimitrov found himself attacking old Socialists and Agrarians who dared criticize independent non-Communist intellectuals who were the most recent recruits to the Fatherland Front. The latter became an institution for ideological discipline and connection with the masses, losing any resemblance to a political coalition. Dimitrov's thinking had evolved from attempts at a united labor front from below to a worker-peasant front with Left Agrarians, to an anti-Fascist Popular Front, to a national Fatherland Front that finally brought him to power. His death in a Russian hospital in 1949 occurred in his second homeland, the country whose arms and victory over fascism he acknowledged had alone made the success of his tactic possible in Bulgaria.[45]

Bibliography

Blagoeva, Stella, *Dimitrov: A Biography*. New York: International Publishers, 1934.

Degras, Jane, ed. *The Communist International, 1919-1943: Documents*. London: Frank Case, 1971.

Drachkovitch, Milorad, and Branko Lazitch (eds.). *The Comintern: Historical Highlights*. New York: Praeger, 1966.

Kosev, D., ed. *Georgi Dimitrov (1882-1972): An Anniversary Collection*. Sofia: Foreign Language Press, 1972.

McKenzie, Kermit. *The Comintern and World Revolution, 1928-1943*. New York: Columbia University Press, 1964.

Oren, Nissan. *Bulgarian Communism: the Road to Power, 1934-1944*. New York: Columbia University Press, 1971.

Panaiotov, Filip. *Along the Road of Georgi Dimitrov*. Sofia: Foreign Language Press, 1963.

Rothschild, Joseph. *The Communist Party of Bulgaria: Origins and Development, 1883-1936*. New York: Columbia University Press, 1959.

Todorov, Kosta. *Balkan Firebrand*. New York: Davis-Zipf, 1943.

English translations of Dimitrov's works:

Dimitroff's Letters from Prison (New York: International Publishers, 1935)

The Working Class Against Fascism (Moscow: Co-operative Publishers, 1935)

The United Front: The Struggle Against Fascism and War (New York: International Publishers, 1938)

The September Uprising, 1923-1953 (Sofia: Nauka i Izkustvo, 1953)

Selected Works, 1910-1949 (Sofia: Foreign Language Press, 1960)

Selected Works (Sofia: Foreign Language Press, 1967).

Bac Ho: Ho Chi Minh
of Vietnam
by Michael Dennis White

Ho Chi Minh was a vigorous exponent of communism, particularly the Communist tenet of anticolonialism. He traveled widely in Europe and Asia before finally returning home to his native Vietnam to lead the struggle for independence that his people waged.

During World War II, Charles Fenn worked for United States intelligence in the Office of Strategic Services.[2] While operating in Southeast Asia, Fenn employed a certain Ho Chi Minh as one of his agents. In his biography of Ho, Fenn noted that he usually analyzed the handwriting of new recruits as a "guide to [their] character," to their dependability as servants of the Allied struggle against Japan. An analysis was made of Ho's handwriting "without any prior concept of the man we were dealing with." Fenn still maintains the accuracy of this handwriting analysis of one of the twentieth century's foremost revolutionaries:

> The essential features are simplicity, desire to make everything clear, remarkable self-control. Knows how to keep a secret. Neat, orderly, unassuming, no interest in dress or outward show. Self-confident and dignified. Gentle but firm. Loyal, sincere and generous, would make a good friend. Outgoing, gets along with anyone. Keen analytical mind, difficult to deceive. Shows readiness to ask questions. Good judge of character. Full of enthusiasm, energy, initiative. Conscientious; painstaking attention to detail. Imaginative, interested in aesthetics, particularly literature. Good sense of humour.
> Faults: diplomatic to the point of contriving. Could be moody and obstinate.[3]

There is double-bladed irony in this graphological analysis. The first cutting edge lies in the fact that this appraisal of Ho's character was commissioned and accepted by military forces of the United States, then an ally to Ho's Vietnamese jungle guerrilllas, but later to become his most powerful military and political foe. Years later many Americans who would willingly wage war against Ho's country could never deny the almost saintlike devotion and self-sacrificing character of this Asian patriot; they would say to themselves and to others, as one American engaged in psychological warfare against the Vietnamese liberation fighters ironically put it, "You know, it's damned difficult to go out and tell people to hate a guy who looks like a half-starved Santa Claus."[4]

The second irony is that at the time the OSS did the study of Ho's handwriting and cooperated with his soldiers, Ho was essentially anonymous to the government of the United States. Likewise, for years he remained much of a mystery to his own people. His fierce dedication to the cause of Vietnamese independence from colonial domination is above reproach. His personal character, his simple life-style, and his stubborn tenacity to his one lifelong ambition of national independence have served as a living symbol to a people wracked with war and shackled by foreign occupation for decades. But for years, despite the clarity of his purpose, biographical details of Ho Chi Minh were obscure.

It is an understatement to say that of all the intelligence reports regarding Vietnam and its people compiled by United States intelligence agencies, this one paragraph is the single most correct assessment of both past and future Vietnam. Its praise of Ho's simplicity, confidence, loyalty, sensitivity, analytical abilities, "enthusiasm, energy, initiative," diplomacy, and (most of all) obstinacy, long ago prophesied the eventual success of Vietnamese revolution and long ago sang the eulogy of foreign hegemony in Southeast Asia.

Nonetheless, in the wake of the recent total military victory of Ho's people, a great deal remains to be said of Ho Chi Minh. The story of "He Who Enlightens" Vietnam must be told. This, then, is the story of Bac Ho, uncle to the nieces and nephews of the future Vietnam.

Ho Chi Minh was one of many pseudonyms of the man originally named Nguyen Sinh Cung.[5] He was born on May 19, 1890, in the village of Hoang Tru and grew up in Kim Lien in the coastal province of central Vietnam.[6] Nghe-An province had been the birthplace of many great patriots and nationalists. Ho, third child of Hoang Thi Loan and Nguyen Sinh Huy, grew up under the shadow of French colonialism. His family was imbued with Nghe-An's tradition of resistance to foreign control. Ho's father received an education in the limited Vietnamese school system and finally, in 1894, entered the mandarin service of the imperial administration.[7] Nguyen had himself participated in the Intellectuals' Rebellion which was crushed by the French in 1888, shortly after they had gained control of their new Asian colony. Because of his opposition to French colonialism, Ho's father was dismissed in 1901 from his minor position by the colonial administration. Although he returned to his small farm in Kim Lien where he taught children and practiced traditional medicine, Nguyen remained a member of one of the various secret organizations committed to the anti-French resistance movement.[8] About this time he renamed his third child, Ho, Nguyen Tat Thanh or Nguyen "Who Will Inevitably Succeed." The father's foresight was like that of a seer.

Ho was ten years old when his mother died. His mother's death seems only to have served as further witness to her third child that life under the French was one of hardship and toil. Corveé labor, increased taxes, compulsory marketing of alcohol, prostitution and opium use, and the degrading poverty and increased misery suffered by his villagers and family at the hands of the French bore heavily on the child's earlier days. His determination to free his country from foreign rule was at this time already deeply embedded in his heart. He was carrying messages for the anti-French underground before he entered the French *lycée* at Vinh, where he was soon dismissed (circa 1905) apparently because of his political activities.[9]

Meanwhile, his sister spent her time stealing French munitions and smuggling them to rebel forces. On several occasions she was jailed for her militant activities. Ho's brother wrote letters of protest against French treatment of the native peoples to the French governor-general. He too was apparently imprisoned for his subversive work, most certainly when he threw to the ground a French official who had kicked him.

In 1905, Ho was enrolled by his father in the French college, Quoc Hoc, in the old imperial capital of Hue. After four years of study, he rebelled against the school's attempts to assimilate Vietnamese culture into French culture and, so, quit the school without his diploma. He found a teaching job in a fishing town not far from Saigon. Shortly after the Chinese nationalist revolution in October, 1911, Ho—who was less an academician and theoretician and more an activist and practitioner—left his job to attend a trade school in Saigon. After three months in a three-year program, he changed his name to Ba and signed aboard the French steamer Latouche-Treville as a galley hand.[10]

Not much is known about Ho's life for the next few years (1912-1916). It appears that he traveled to France where he worked for a short time as a family servant in Le Havre. He seems to have made contact with some of his father's revolutionary friends who belonged to the League for Human Rights. He returned to the sea, apparently revisting Saigon where he had an argument with his father after which the two never saw each other again. It is reported that Ho, sailing from Vietnam, traveled to America and a number of French colonies. From his tour of the world, Ho observed a very important truth: colonialism, whether under French rule, British rule, *et alii,* whether in Senegal, India, Tunis, South Africa, *et multi alii,* was everywhere the worst, most disgusting, and violent form of exploitation on the face of the earth. Once after seeing four Africans drown during a storm as they tried to get a line ashore to save all on board Ho's boat, he remarked, "To the colonialists the life of an Asian is not worth a cent. . . . They [French officers] burst out laughing while our compatriots died for their sake."[11]

Sometime thereafter, Ho journeyed to London where, to survive, he shoveled snow for London city schools, worked as a boiler tender in a boardinghouse, washed dishes, and finally was promoted as an assistant to a rather renowned chef at the Carlton Hotel. It was in England that Ho made his first significant political contacts in Europe, with the Chinese and Indian Overseas Work-

ers' Association, an anticolonialist and anti-imperialist organization. It is also rumored that he met with Irish nationalists on a
journey to Liverpool shortly before the Easter Rising of 1916.
Yet, in spite of these experiences, Ho was still not the Communist he eventually became. Subsequent events led him to that
eventuality.

The first of those crucial events came in 1917 when he
went to France. By that time, the first of the world wars was in
its third year, and France was reeling from the German onslaught.
In order to maintain its defense perimeters, France began to con-
script Annamites (Vietnamese). Over eighty thousand Vietnamese were forcibly drafted and brought to France, either to work
in war factories or fight at the front alongside French "citizens."
Herein lay the second lesson of Ho's world travels. Vietnamese
slaves served alongside French men and women, the very people
who colonized their country. The work of the Vietnamese was the
same as that of the French; the pay was much the same; the hours
and responsibilities were identical. Moreover, Vietnamese serving
as military police had even been ordered to fire upon mutinous
French troops in 1917. As one journalist wrote, "The myth of
the all-powerful and all-knowing white master, so assiduously
fostered overseas by the colonial administration, was exactly that:
a myth."[12] But for Ho Chi Minh that incident meant more than
the destruction of the myth of white superiority. Intuitively he
understood that the myth of white superiority was based on a
more important myth: that of the supposed social harmony and
political unity of all white peoples. Ho now perceived that this
false unity belied the truth that the populations of the mother
countries of colonialism were themselves divided into classes with
competing and antagonistic interests. The vast majority of the
French people had little in common with the interests of colonial
administrators. Ho believed that a distinction must be made between French masters and French servants. As he put it in simple, sometimes laconic, fashion: "The French in France are good;
it is the French colonialists who are cruel and inhuman."[13] This
perceptive observation served Ho well in future years, for, unlike
some fervent natonalists, Ho harbored no racial hatred toward the
French.[14] His ability to make simple but accurate analytical dis-

tinctions such as this later enabled him to win support from French people in his fight for Vietnamese independence, and to ally and work with some French during decisive moments of the national liberation struggle against Japan, the Kuomintang of China, the post-World War II French Republic, and, finally, America.

Upon arriving in Paris, Ho took still another name. To his family name Nguyen, he added Ai Quoc, which means "love one's country." For the next fifteen year the name Nguyen the Patriot would feed, like wood a fire, the bloodlust of the dreaded French *Sûreté,* or secret police.

Ho found work retouching photographs and painting so-called Chinese antiquities that had been made in France.[15] But his real purpose in France was to recruit and organize the many Vietnamese conscripts for the struggle against French colonial rule. He had only been living in France for a short time when news came of the October Revolution of the Bolshevik (Communist) party in Russia. Ho later wrote:

> At that time, I supported the October Revolution only instinctively, not yet grasping all its historic importance. I loved and admired Lenin because he was a great patriot who liberated his country; until then, I had read none of his books.
> [I later joined the French Socialist party because these comrades] had shown their sympathy towards me, towards the struggle of the oppressed peoples. But I understood neither what was a party, a trade union, nor what was socialism nor communism.[16]

Ho began to study what he did not understand. He went to Socialist meetings, attended study groups, and involved himself in a variety of political education projects. He founded the Inter-colonial Union (or the League of Colonial Peoples) and with a compatriot, Nguyen The Truyen, published its journal, *Le Paria* (The Outcast). Their first major treatise was *French Colonization on Trial,* after which they published *Viet Nam Hon* (The Soul of Vietnam), a work which continued the attack of *Le Paria* on Western colonial policy. His understanding of Communist theory grew as his association with French Marxists deepened. Socialist Léon Blum, later premier of France; Paul Vaillant-Courtier, editor of the famous Communist newspaper *l'Humanité*; and Charles Longuet, nephew of Karl Marx and editor of *Le Populaire* were but a few of those with whom he worked and from whom he learned so much during the formative period of his early Socialist experience.

But the most decisive moment in Ho's life, with regard to his decision to become a Communist, occurred in the midst of his political studies when he read Lenin's "Thesis on the National and Colonial Questions." His reaction to this theoretical work was decisive to the destiny of the Vietnamese people.

> There were political terms difficult to understand in this thesis. But by dint of reading it again and again, finally I could grasp the main part of it. What emotion, enthusiasm, clearsightedness, and confidence it instilled in me! I wept for joy. Though sitting alone in my room, I shouted out aloud as if addressing large crowds: "Dear martyrs, compatriots! This is what we need, this is the path to our liberation!"
> After that I had entire confidence in Lenin, in the Third International.[17]

Patriotism had led Ho to communism; nationalism, he concluded, was the foundation for true internationalism. Once enslaved, colonized countries were made fully independent from the domination of the major industrial powers of the world, and the possibility of successful working-class revolutions in capitalist nations was practically ensured. Ho, with his great faith in human potential, finally freed from class stratification and conflicting class interests, held firmly to the belief that human beings might effectively cooperate in the productive life and political decision-making processes which play a major role in determining the quality of human life. From the labor of national liberation and proletariat revolution would be born a true and lasting internationalism, a permanent world peace based on principle to replace the temporary periods of peace established between nations only as a matter of strategic and tactical policies.

As his maturation as a Communist continued, World War I came to an end. In 1917, the victorious Allied powers assembled at Versailles, where the colonies became the victors' spoils to be divided among them. Under the principles of Woodrow Wilson's Fourteen Points and the right of every nation to self-determination, the Western Allies essentially carved up the map of the world as if it were a turkey dinner on Thanksgiving Day. The competing interests of Britain, France, Italy, and the United States served some nations, or pseudonations, in good stead. But no advocate could be found to defend the interests of Vietnam. For days on end, Ho stood outside the conference doors of Versailles trying to submit for consideration his petition on behalf of the colonized "Annamites." Today the eight points of his proposal seem a very "liberal" or moderate solution to the major problems facing his country in 1919. His demands did not even include the complete independence of Vietnam. Instead, he sought: (1) amnesty for all political prisoners; (2) equal rights for Vietnamese and French in Indochina; (3) freedom of the press; (4) freedom of association and assembly; (5) freedom to travel; (6) more schools and equal opportunity to study; (7) abolition of colonial rule by judgments and decree, with the institution of duly enacted laws; and (8) appointment of a Vietnamese delegation to protect Vietnamese interests by advising and consulting with the French government.

The Western governments chose to ignore Ho and his proposals, a choice they must surely regret in retrospect. They scoffed at what they considered to be Ho's audacity. Vietnamese, however, first learned of Ho and never forgot his courage to publicly condemn French colonization while he stood in the belly of the beast, in France itself. As one fellow nationalist who met Ho in France recounted: "Suddenly the imperialists were faced with the claims . . . made by Ho Chi Minh. The French called it a bomb. We called it a thunderbolt. We were overjoyed. How could any of us refrain from admiring the man who stood up so courageously to make claims on our behalf?"[18] Ho Chi Minh's acts gained him a large measure of popularity.

The rejection of his petition at Versailles disappointed Ho, but it did not discourage him. He learned a great, if terrible, lesson. Vietnamese independence would never be a gift from the foreign French power. Self-determination could not be given by another; it must be taken by the self and fashioned in its own image. The Vietnamese would have to fight for their independence. The price for winning their self-determination would be dear, of this Ho had no doubts. But in the end the precious victory of freedom would be even more dear than a gift outright.

Ho's fate as a Communist patriot was sealed. In December 1920 he attended the Eighteenth National Congress of the French Socialist party at Tours. He came to Tours armed with the knowledge that the newly formed Third International under the leadership of Lenin and the Russian Communist party fully endorsed and supported the organization of the colonial peoples and the proletariat of the Western metropolises. The Third International had, in September 1920, convoked the Congress of the Oriental People in Baku. As Ho wrote four years later, "For the first time (at Baku), the proletariat of the conquering Western states and that of the subject Eastern countries fraternally joined hands and deliberated in common on the best means to defeat their common enemy, imperialism."[19]

A major debate occurred at the Tours Congress over whether the French Socialist party should remain a member of the Second International or join the Third under Lenin. The Second International had come to represent a policy of compromise and cooperation with the bourgeoisie. Their position was defended by pointing to the recent failures of Communist revolutions in Europe.. The Third International advocated a policy of continued opposition to and subversion of the bourgeois states. Their counterargument was that the recent European revolutions had failed precisely because the Socialist parties had failed to act decisively in leading and supporting the revolts. The basically nonrevolutionary policy of the Socialists—i.e., their hesitancy to completely oppose the bourgeoisie—had resulted in a terrible setback for the working-class movement.

Ho spoke at Tours, and pleaded with the Socialists: "[You] must act practically to support the oppressed natives." Ai Quoc was not satisfied when Longuet, a relative of Karl Marx, lamely excused himself by saying, "I have spoken in favor of the natives." Such words were no longer enough for Ho. He had heard them from the bourgeoisie at Versailles; he did not want to hear them from the Socialists at Tours. Finally, on December 30, 1920, Ho rose to address the Congress:

> I understand very well one single thing: The Third International concerns itself a great deal with the colonial question. Its delegates promise to help the oppressed colonial peoples to regain their

liberty and independence. The adherents of the Second International have not said a word about the fate of the colonial areas.[20]

At Tours, Ho voted with the left-wing Socialists to join the Third International.[21] He, a Vietnamese, had just become a founding member of the French Communist party. The loyal nationalist became an equally devoted agent of internationalism. In 1921, he drafted the Manifesto of the Intercolonial Union, modeled after the *Communist Manifesto* of 1848, wherein he addressed his "brothers of the colonies . . . and oppressed brothers of the metropolitan countries" and urged them to unite in opposition to imperialism, which served the interests of none but the bourgeoisie.[22]

In 1922, Ho attended the Comintern (Communist Third International) meetings in Moscow. He returned to Moscow in 1923 to attend the Krestintern (Peasant International) and again in 1924 to speak to the Fifth Comintern Congress. Consistently he reminded the world Communists of Lenin's pledge to the colonies and of their duty to support colonial struggles against imperialism.

Later, in 1924, Ho went to China with a Russian mission to help train the Chinese Republican Army, then under the leadership of Chiang Kai-shek. Ho served the civilian representative of the mission, Michael Borodin, as secretary-interpreter. He adopted other pseudonyms, Vuong and Song Man Tcho, and proceeded to organize the many Vietnamese exiles living in China. He established a Vietnam Revolutionary Youth League and League of Oppressed Asian Peoples to train a cadre who would reinfiltrate Vietnam and organize strikes of the anti-French resistance. In this work, Ho became friends with Pham Van Dong, later to be prime minister of North Vietnam.

In 1927, Chiang Kai-shek turned on the Communists and massacred tens of thousands. Ho escaped to Russia where he was given new duties. He was first sent to the Congress Against Imperialist War in Brussels (attended by Nehru and Madame Sun Yat-sen) and then to France, Germany, Italy, and Switzerland. Then, in early 1930, assuming another name, Thau Chin, so as to elude the French *Sûreté,* he joined the South Asiatic Bureau of the Comintern in Bangkok where thousands of Vietnamese refu-

gees fled in the wake of repression in China and their own homeland. In Siam, Ho established a school, founded a peasant coop-
erative and issued a newsletter. Suddenly, in the midst of this
work, he was ordered to Hong Kong to settle disputes among the
factionalized Indochinese Communists.

The first Indochinese Communist party had been formed in
northern Vietnam in June 1929. A second (the Annamese Communist party) and a third (the Tan Tiet, or Indochina Communist
League) were founded several months later. Rival sectarianism
had prevented all three groups from becoming a genuinely effective
revolutionary organization in southeast Asia. The Executive Committee of the Comintern recognized the need for unity, and thus
sent Ho to convene a unity conference and mediate the differences
among the three parties. The conference took place in a crowded
Hong Kong stadium during a bitterly contested soccer game. The
setting provided convenient (and, in retrospect, humorous) cover
for the conference participants. From this meeting emerged a
single unified party, Viet Nam Cong San Dong, later renamed the
Indochinese Communist party (ICP), determined to overthrow
French colonialism and establish the complete independence of
Indochina. (Later that year the ICP's only major rival, the
VNQDD or Vietnamese Nationalist party, was crushed by the
French in an abortive insurrection. The ICP remained the only
strong revolutionary party in Vietnam.)

Ho continued to travel throughout southern Asia, disguised
as Chinese businessman Tong Van So. On June 5, 1931, he was
arrested by the British in Hong Kong. The *Sûreté* sought
his extradition, for in Vinh, capital of his native province, Ho
had been sentenced to death *in absentia* by a French tribunal for
his subversive activities against the French Republic. But Britain,
although rounding up subversives in Hong Kong, was not eager to
oblige the French government. There are conflicting accounts of
this matter, but Ho was eventually imprisoned. Then, a British
doctor discovered that he had tuberculosis of the lungs, so he was
tran-ferred to a prison hospital. Again, details are garbled. but
somehow, for whatever reason, with whatever support from either
the hospital staff or British intelligence, Ho's escape was arranged
in autumn 1932.[23] A cover-up story was released, indicating that

he had died. All around the world, in the Soviet press and in *l'Humanité,* it was reported that Ho was dead. The grief was manifest in the Communist and Vietnamese nationalist movements. In the offices of the French *Sûreté,* the file on Ho Chi Minh was closed with the simple notation: "Died in the Hongkong gaol."[24]

Again a shroud of mystery blankets Ho's life. Some say he married during this time and even had a daughter. Others report that for a time he fell out of favor with the Soviet government as a result of the temporary collapse of the ICP and the mass arrests of its membership. At any rate, in 1934 he was finally smuggled through Shanghai into Russia. There he attended the Lenin School, which trained important Communist cadres. This was a troubled time in the Soviet Union. Stalin was waging war against Trotsky and his followers. Ho was not purged, perhaps because he was "a 'doer' rather than a theoretician."[25]

At the Seventh Comintern Congress Ho (under yet another name) spoke in favor of the foundation of a Popular Front, composed of Communists and non-Communist anti-Fascists, to stem the tide of burgeoning European fascism. This United Front policy, known as the "Dimitrov Line," had not yet been adopted by the ICP. Ho was dispatched to Indochina to guide the ICP in the implementation of the United Front policy. Even for Ho this policy must have been a tough pill to swallow, for it meant cooperation with the French regime (and noncooperation with Trotskyists who had been among his former allies).

Then, in 1939, Moscow signed a nonaggression pact with Germany. Threatened by this political turnabout, the French government outlawed the French Communist party and hunted down members of the ICP. The Central Committee of the ICP retreated to China. Ho also moved to China where he served in a guerrilla unit of the Chinese Eighth Route Army.[26] In June 1940, Germany invaded France and won a swift victory. The French Republic fell, and French Colonialists were overwhelmed and disoriented by the defeat of their nation. The Colonialists quickly moved to appease Japan and essentially surrendered Indochina to the Japanese in August 1940. The Vietnamese also moved quickly in a premature rebellion against the Fascists. Ho had opposed armed insurrection at that time, but his warning

came too late to forestall the rebellion. Although initially successful, the guerrillas were soon crushed by the French Vichy government (French collaborators with the German Nazis) with the assistance of Japanese troops.

In November 1940, a base of operations was established in
a Chinese town adjacent to the Vietnamese border. From this base
Ho entered Vietnam for the first time in thirty years. He quar-
tered himself in a cave where, on May 19, 1941 (his fifty-first
birthday), the Viet Nam Doc Lap Dong (League for Vietnamese
Independence or Vietminh) was born. On June 6, 1941, Ho ap-
pealed to all patriots: "Revolutionary fighters, the time for liberation has come! Let's hold high the banner of independence, and
lead the whole people in the fight to destroy the common enemy.
. . . Let the entire people march forward! Let us all unite and
drive out the French and Japanese!"[27]

With the founding of the Vietminh and the inauguration of a
full-fledged war for national liberation, Ho himself became less an
agent for the Comintern and more an "independent adjutant."[28]
It was his longing for Vietnamese independence which had first
brought Ho to communism. In spite of (or because of) his activ-
ism for internationalism, he now decided to work primarily for his
own country's liberation. Never again would he travel on behalf
of the Soviet Union or the Comintern. His journeys would be for
the sake of his own nation.

In August 1942, he made his first such journey to China to
organize support from Vietnamese in China and to request assistance from the anti-Japanese Kuomintang. On this trip he took
his last and most famous name of Ho Chi Minh. His mission was
anything but a success. On August 28, 1942, Ho was arrested
by one of Chiang Kai-shek's military governors on charges that
he was a French Vichy spy. Thirteen months later, Ho was released from prison for reasons which have never been made
explicit.

The next year and a half was difficult for the Vietminh, but
even more difficult for Ho Chi Minh personally. He was often
seriously ill, once near death as he lapsed into a coma. But the
hope of independence gave him strength. Hardship steeled his
determination. In May 1945, an ICP and People's Congresses

were held in Tuyen Quang province. A provisional government was founded and Ho Chi Minh was chosen president. Preparations were made for the expansion of guerrilla warfare and a general uprising. All armed forces were merged into the Liberation Army.

Then, during the confusion caused by the surrender of the Japanese, the freedom fighters struck. Within ten days, the Vietminh had seized power in their own country. On August 29, the identity of the leader of the new government was officially announced. Ho Chi Minh was reintroduced to the hearts of his people as the former Nguyen Ai Quoc, Nguyen the Patriot, "who had devoted his whole life to achieving his country's independence."[29] His name was a rallying cry for freedom and independence. "In less than a week, nearly the whole population was referring to him affectionately as 'Uncle,'" the unmarried adult who cared for all the children.[30]

On September 2, 1945, in Hanoi, Ho Chi Minh read the historic Declaration of Independence (modeled after America's own Declaration). By January 6, 1946, general elections were held for a new National Assembly; two months later the assembly adopted the first constitution for independent Vietnam.

For the next three decades the struggle to maintain that right to independence continued. France attacked the first independent Socialist nation of far Asia on November 23, 1946. In January 1950, first the People's Republic of China and then the Soviet Union recognized Ho's Democratic Republic of Vietnam. Still, the war dragged on until the French, supported by United States' payments of eighty percent of their costs, were defeated at the siege of Dien Bien Phu in 1954.

The Geneva Conference (begun on the day of the French defeat) resulted in the temporary partition of Vietnam into two zones pending general elections to be held by July 1956. Ho Chi Minh waited patiently but futilely for the fulfillment of these and other Geneva agreements. After this betrayal, the war began again, this time against the United States. That government sent half a million troops to Vietnam and it took the war to Hanoi with air bombing raids. War continued during five years of negotiations between the two countries. Ho, "the leader and soul of the people's effort and resistance,"[31] died at the age of seventy-nine before all United States military forces were withdrawn from southern Vietnam and before, in the spring of 1975, his troops defeated the rulers of the south and entered Saigon victoriously.

But his work was completed and his prophecy of August 1945 was fulfilled:

> Our country won't be automatically independent when the Japanese are defeated. Many difficulties and obstacles will crop up. We must be wise and resolute. We must be wise to avoid things that may prove disadvantageous to us. We must be resolute to win complete independence. In the world, after this war [World War II], a people who are resolute and unanimous in demanding independence are sure to be independent. We shall be victorious.[32]

Ho Chi Minh was an exemplary revolutionary of the twentieth century. As Vietnamese Premier Pham Van Dong said on the eightieth anniversary of Ho's birth, "He is the symbol of our nation, conscience of our time."[33] Pham also said of Ho:

> His life is a shining example of revolutionary heroism, militant solidarity, simplicity, modesty, industry, thrift, uprightness, integrity, total dedication to the public interest, and complete selflessness. He has been closely associated with the splendid successes of the Vietnamese revolution ever since our Party came into being, and his name personifies the most glorious epoch in the history of the Vietnamese nation.[34]

Ho's tenacity to his aims, his perseverance in the midst of eight decades of adversity and threats to his life, were nothing short of remarkable. As Fidel Castro and Cuba's president, Osvaldo Dorticos, said: "Never on such a narrow strip of land, in such a short time, has taken place such a struggle decisive to the future of mankind as that led by Ho Chi Minh . . . the indomitable fortress of the world revolutionary struggle. . . ."[35]

Ho's life and his style of work were marked by an unusual simplicity. Recalling his first meeting with Ho, Vo Nguyen Giap, the leading general of the national liberation struggle, remarked, "I found in him that simplicity of manner, that lucidity of character, which later, when I worked by his side, always had the same impact on me."[36] Before the August revolution his "office" was a cave, his "desk" a flat rock, his "bed" branches.[37] After the revolution, his humble way of living changed little. He lived in one small room in the former servants' quarters of the former French governor-general's palace in Hanoi. Once a correspondent asked if he might take a photo of Ho at work in his office. Ho replied, with a smile, 'But I don't have an office. If it is fine, I work out in the garden; if it rains I work on the verandah and if it is cold, I work in my room."[38] This simplicity, this exemplary frugality and modesty was with him to the end, when he wrote in his last testament: "When I am gone, grand funerals should be avoided in order not to waste the people's time and money."[39]

Ho's thoughts were simple, too, for his goal was simple:

> I have had only one aim in life: to struggle for the good of the country and well-being of my people. It is for this reason that I have had to hide in the mountains, crouch in prisons. Whatever the moment, whatever the place, I have had a single aim, the interest of the nation, the good of the people. . . .
>
> About personal matters—all my life, I have served the fatherland, the revolution, and the people with all my heart and strength. If I should now depart from this world, I would have nothing to regret, except not being able to serve longer and more. . . .[40]

Ho was not a critical theorist like Marx, Lenin, Lukacs, Luxemburg, and so many other intellectual Communists. But he always managed to link theory with practice in a simple but clearsighted fashion. He reduced complex questions and situations to their profound elements, and explained them in fundamentally intelligible ways. Ho was a perceptive realist and a scholar of practice. With clarity, he refashioned old, traditional concepts of Vietnamese culture so as to mold a revolutionary spirit in the modern twentieth century. As he declared, he drew upon history to shape the future: "When I was young, I studied Buddhism, Confucianism, Christianity, as well as Marxism. There is something good in each doctrine."[41] With this sensitivity, Ho persuaded the peasant villagers to adopt new values and to engage in a novel style of mass political involvement by making simply relevant the "homely images" and familiar traditions.[42]

Gentleness did not prevent Ho from being straightforward in criticisms of his comrades' not-so-simple practice. After Giap had produced a lithographed newspaper, Ho told him, with a smile:

"We have received your paper but I didn't read it, nor did the other comrades. Your articles were long and unintelligible."[43]

To the end of his life this patriot was a Communist. Unlike some, he had walked the tightrope between the growing antagonism between the Soviet Union and the People's Republic of China. His appreciation and affection for the support offered by the people of these Socialist lands caused him to urge his own party to "do its best to contribute effectively to the restoration of unity among the fraternal parties on the basis of Marxism-Leninism and proletarian internationalism, in a way which conforms to both reason and sentiment."[44]

On September 3, 1969, Ho Chi Minh died after a serious heart attack. But he left "an extremely precious legacy." The Vietnamese Workers' party, the descendant of the ICP, paid its *Last Tribute* to Ho when it wrote: "This is the Ho Chi Minh epoch, the most brilliant one in our nation's glorious history. This is the era of independence and freedom for the Fatherland, the era of socialism in our country."[45]

Bibliography

Burchett, Wilfred. *Ho Chi Minh: An Appreciation*. New York: The Guardian, 1972.

Chesneaux, Jean. *Days with Ho Chi Minh*. Hanoi: Foreign Languages Publishing House, 1965.

Chomsky, Noam. *American Power and the New Mandarins*. New York: Vintage Books, 1967.

Committee of Concerned Asian Scholars. *The Indochina Story*. New York: Bantam Books, 1970.

Devillers, Philippe. "Vietnamese Nationalism and French Policies." In W. L. Holland, ed., *Asian Nationalism and the West*. New York: Macmillan Co., 1953.

Effros, William G., comp. *Quotations Vietnam: 1945-1970*. New York: Random House, 1970.

Eisenhower, Dwight D. *Mandate for Change*. New York: Doubleday, 1963.

Fall, Bernard. *Last Reflections on a War*. New York: Schoken Books, 1972.

Fenn, Charles. *Ho Chi Minh: A Biographical Introduction*. New York: Charles Scribner's Sons, 1973.

Fitzgerald, Frances. *Fire in the Lake: The Vietnamese and the Americans in Vietnam*. Boston: Little, Brown, 1972.

Halberstam, David. *Ho*. New York: Random House, 1971.

Hammer, Ellen J. *The Struggle for Indochina*. Stanford: Stanford University Press, 1954.

Ho Chi Minh. *Prison Diary*. Translated by Aileen Palmer. Hanoi: Foreign Languages Publishing House, 1962.

Ho Chi Minh. *Ho Chi Minh on Revolution: Selected Writings, 1920-1966*. Edited by Bernard B. Fall. New York: Praeger, 1967.

Ho Chi Minh. *Selected Articles and Speeches, 1920-1967*. Edited by Jack Woodis. London: Lawrence and Wishart Ltd., 1969.

Hoang Van Chi. *From Colonialism to Communism: A Case History of North Vietnam*. New York: Praeger, 1964.

Lacouture, Jean. *Ho Chi Minh: A Political Biography*. Translated by Peter Wiles. New York: Random House, 1968.

Lancaster, Donald. *The Emancipation of French Indochina*. New York: Oxford University Press, 1961.

Le Than Khoi, *Le Viet-Nam; Historie et Civilisation.* Paris: Les Editions de Minuit, 1955.

McAlister, John T., Jr. *Vietnam; The Origins of Revolution.* New York: Alfred A. Knopf, 1969.

Mohan Das, S. R. *Ho Chi Minh: Nationalist or Soviet Agent?* Bombay: Democratic Research Service, 1951.

Mus, Paul. "Cultural Backgrounds of Present Problems," *Asia* (Winter, 1966), pp. 10-21.

Mus, Paul. "The Unaccountable Mr. Ho," *New Journal,* May 12, 1968, p. 9.

Mus, Paul. *Vietnam: Sociologie d'une Guerre.* Paris: Editions du Seuil, 1952.

N. Khac Huyen. *Vision Accomplished? The Enigma of Ho Chi Minh.* New York: Macmillan, 1971.

Neumann-Hoditz, Reinhold. *Portrait of Ho Chi Minh.* Translated by John Hargreaves. New York: Herder and Herder, 1972.

Pham Van Dong and the Committee for the Study of the History of the Vietnamese Workers' Party. *Our President: Ho Chi Minh.* Hanoi: Foreign Languages Publishing House, 1970.

Sainteny, Jean. *Ho Chi Minh and His Vietnam: A Personal Memoir.* Translated by Herma Briffault. Chicago: Cowles, 1972.

Shaplen, Robert. *The Lost Revolution.* London: Andre Deutch, 1966.

Sontag, Susan. *Trip to Hanoi.* New York: Farrar, Straus and Giroux, 1968.

Thich Nhat Hanh. *Vietnam: Lotus in a Sea of Fire.* New York: Hill and Wang, 1967.

Thompson, Virginia. *French Indochina.* New York: Macmillan, 1937.

Tran Dan Tien. *Glimpses of the Life of Ho Chi Minh.* Hanoi: Foreign Languages Publishing House, 1958.

Truong Buu Lam. *Patterns of Vietnamese Response to Foreign Intervention: 1858-1900.* Monograph Series No. 11. New Haven, Conn.: Southeast Asia Studies, Yale University, 1967.

Truong Chinh, (Dang Xuan Khu). *President Ho Chi Minh: Beloved Leader of the Vietnamese People.* Hanoi: Foreign Languages Publishing House, 1966.

Truong Chinh (Dang Xuan Khu). *The August Revolution.* Hanoi: Foreign Languages Publishing House, 1958.

Vo Nguyen Giap. *People's War, People's Army: The Viet Cong Insurrection Manual for Underdeveloped Countries.* New York: Praeger, 1962.

Warner, Dennis. *The Last Confucian.* Harmondsworth, England: Penguin Books, 1963.

Weiss, Peter. *Note on the Cultural Life of the Democratic Republic of Vietnam.* New York: Dell, 1970.

Chapter 4

Marxism and Democracy

Lucio Colletti on Socialism and Democracy
by Norman Fischer

Lucio Colletti, the Italian Marxist philosopher, connects Marxism and democracy by utilizing the thought of Rousseau, Marx, and Lenin. For him these thinkers interpret democracy as the active rule of the people, a rule which is opposed to the power of the state. This tradition of democracy leads to egalitarian attitudes toward property. Colletti is opposed to another attitude toward democracy both within and without the Marxist movement. The exponents of this view are Locke, the German Social Democrats, and the followers of Stalin. In Locke's view, democracy simply means the guarantee by the state that people will be treated equally. This does not stress the active role of the people in opposition to the state. Similarly, the German Social Democrats thought that socialism would be given by the state. Stalinism is characterized also by an acceptance of the importance of the state, as well as by occasional contempt for even the minimally democratic thought of Locke.

Contemporary Italian thought offers a wide array of discussions on the subject of the relation between socialism and democracy.[1] The recent wave of translations in French, English, and German of the work of Lucio Colletti, the Italian Marxist philosopher, is one index of the international significance of this topic. The following essay presents an analysis of the achievements and limitations of Colletti's work on socialism and the political theory of democracy.

Colletti has constructed a theory of democracy which cuts across three thinkers and four separate texts: Rousseau's *The Social Contract* (1762), Marx's *Critique of Hegel's Doctrine of the*

State (1843), Marx's *The Civil War in France* (1871), and Lenin's *The State and Revolution* (1917). For Colletti, these writings represent the trajectory of the most progressive aspects of democratic theory from several decades before the French revolution to the time of the Russian revolution. He contrasts this account of democracy with another one which he locates most prominently in Locke's *The Second Treatise of Government* (1690). The difference between the two traditions is that the former sees democracy, or Socialist democracy, as something taken by the people, whereas the latter sees democracy as something given by the state. Colletti goes on to use this distinction to analyze some of the major trends in socialism in the late nineteenth and twentieth centuries, judging them by whether they follow the line from Rousseau, Marx, and Lenin; whether they follow the Lockian tradition; or whether they don't even attempt to construct a democratic socialism. Lenin's original practical vision of what the Russian revolution should be is an example of the first; German social democracy at the end of the nineteenth and the beginning of the twentieth centuries is an example of the second; and Stalinism is a combination of the second and the third.

Colletti argues that the basic links between Rousseau, Marx, and Lenin are: (1) their attack on the representative state, the state where the people elect representatives to make their laws and act for them, and then passively accept the result; (2) their notion that what government there is should be constantly subjected to the possibility of being recalled; (3) the desirability of the shrinking and even the disappearance of the state.[2] For Colletti, these are the cornerstones of and criteria for an adequate democratic theory and Rousseau is their originator. The genius of Marx and Lenin was to place them within a specific economic and social context. In doing this, they were able to apply the concept of democracy to socialism.

A short account of certain doctrines from Rousseau's *The Social Contract* will suffice to show the prima facie case for the significance that Colletti assigns to him.[3] Rousseau uses the term "democracy" in such a way that it would not have to and probably would not apply when only the first two criteria are being met. When they are met, a republic exists. Furthermore, if the first two are not met, a republic does not exist and, if all three are not met, then a democratic republic does not exist. Rousseau's analysis relates to the three cornerstones in the following way. First, he criticizes the representative state by arguing that the people themselves must make all the laws. They cannot elect legislators to do that for them. They can elect a government, but it simply has the task of executing the laws. The center of moral authority is in the legislative rather than the executive branch. Second, he argues that at any time the people, as the legislative body, can recall the officers of the government. Third, a republic becomes a democratic republic if all the people not only make the laws, but also execute them, and thus do away with government as a body separate from the people. This would entail the disappearance of the state if the latter is identified with Rousseau's "government." Rousseau, it should be noted, was confident that a republic could be attained but had more doubts about the possibility of creating a democratic republic.

Democracy for Rousseau, then, would be identical with his democratic republic and entails the existence of all three conditions. Since this is an overly narrow and idiosyncratic use of "democracy," I will also use "democracy" to refer to the attainment of the first two conditions, although for Rousseau this would only be a republic and not a democratic republic. Such a widening of the term "democracy" is more advisable in that these two conditions are interconnected in themselves and separable from the third. For it would be difficult to criticize the representative state without having some mechanism for recalling the executive body. Yet both of these conditions could be attained without all of the people being the executive body; and discussion of how to attain these conditions constitutes contribution to a theory of democracy.

Rousseau elaborates the first two criteria by connecting the revocability of government officials and the necessity of all the people making the laws with the social contract theory. In his version of this theory, the people agree about how they should rule their lives and never give this power to anyone else. They have a government for efficiency, but it is constantly under their control. This social contract, however, must not be seen as simply a purified version of the idea of democracy that has become the most common in contemporary understanding, i.e., that democracy consists in majority rule. Indeed, it is true that once the contract has been instituted, then the majority does decide what laws will be made and the minority, although it gets to vote for these laws, still must accept the will of the majority when it loses. However, there are two differences between Rousseau's theory and typical majority rule theories. First, the original decision to set up the contract among the people must not be made by a simple majority, but must rather be unanimous. Second, the people must accept certain basic moral principles, otherwise the contract is worthless.

If we use democracy, then, to refer to the attainment of Colletti's first two conditions, we see that for Rousseau it entails three other conditions: (1) there must be initial unanimous agreement on the nature of what people want from their political society; (2) after that, laws are made by the majority; and (3) the people must commit themselves to certain basic moral principles.

It is this last condition which has been at the center of the debate over Rousseau's theory of democracy. In particular, people have asked what these basic principles are. It seems, however, that the basic one is equality; whether there are others equally important is a question that would take us too far afield.[4]

Rousseau's novelty, then, consists in the idea that for democracy to exist the majority must accept the principle of equality. This notion, however, entails what I call the paradox of democracy.

Rousseau's theory entails the view that the majority can fail to have the moral principle of equality and thus can fail to perform just and right actions. It also entails the view, however, that although the minority may at some time have this commitment to democracy, nevertheless if it uses this commitment to create an elite minority government, then it, too, fails to be right. This is the paradox of democracy. If only the few have committed themselves to equality and if the majority make decisions, then it is impossible for anyone to act democratically. Thus, Rousseau's theory gives no easy solutions. When commitment to equality is divorced from mass action, then all political actions performed in that situation will be imperfect. Nevertheless, political actions must be performed, but they must have as their ultimate aim the ending of the split between equality and majority rule. Awareness of this split gives humility to the democratic man. Knowing that he will sometimes act in imperfect circumstances he will be particularly careful to guard against a state of mind that accepts those circumstances as permanently given. Also that humility and hope for the future will prevent him from adopting forms of psychological authoritarianism that tend to be fostered in undemocratic circumstances.

Now one problem with Colletti's account is that although he recognizes that Rousseau is concerned with common interests and principles, he does not deal adequately with how this is connected with the mass action criterion for democracy. This raises problems for his interpretation of his classical democratic text number two: Marx's *Critique of Hegel's Doctrine of the State.*[5] For this work, although containing many economic insights and many foreshadowings of the theory of socialism and its relation to democracy, must also be looked at in the context of a philosophical debate in nineteenth-century Germany between various interpretations of commitment to moral principles.

The German philosophers debated over which principles to adopt, where the principles came from, and whether the principles should be more common to everyone or more unique to each person. Sometimes this debate was directly political in nature but sometimes, as in Ludwig Feuerbach, little direct interest was shown in man's political institutions. In Marx's *Critique* he basically takes the side of Feuerbach versus Hegel in a debate where the former had accused the latter of stressing that the principles should come from the state. Against this, Feuerbach had argued that the principles should come from men expressing their societal and common interests naturally rather than through the state. Although Feuerbach once called this state of things communistic he did not attempt to elaborate the situation in any practical detail.[6] Such practical details are also lacking for the most part in Marx's *Critique.*

It is true, on the other hand, that Colletti is certainly right to find in that work evidence of the first and third cornerstones: the critique of the representative state and the disappearance of the state. But it is more questionable whether the second corner-

stone, the revocable delegates of the people, is really there.
Indeed, Marx's account in this work is much less political than
Rousseau's. Rousseau, for example, talks of how the commitment
to the principle of equality will be expressed in law, whereas
Marx seems to suggest that in the truly democratic society there
will be neither politics nor law. What is positive in Colletti's
account of this text is that he sees how, even in this early statement, Marx views socialism as the free and active participation
of individuals. What is not so positive is that he tends to assimilate
Marx's attitude toward politics and law into Rousseau's belief that
the two should be transformed rather than abolished. The problem
is that Colletti himself stresses the negation rather than the
transformation of politics and law. Fortunately Colletti's third
classical text, Marx's *Civil War in France,* presents an account of
socialism, politics, and democracy which is much more elaborate
than that found in Rousseau or in Marx's *Critique of Hegel's
Doctrine of the State.*

There is no doubt that in *The Civil War in France* Marx
stresses all three of Colletti's cornerstones of democracy, most
famously the disappearance of the state. The disappearance of
the state in socialism does not entail, however, that politics and
law will also disappear. The argument that it does could only
be made by simply equating the state with politics and law or
else by arguing that the state is a necessary and sufficient condition for politics and law. Both positions can be shown to be
fallacious if one is willing to accept the following definitions of
state, law, and politics.

Laws are publicly observable and codified moral rules.
Politics is the use of laws to facilitate agreements among men.
The state exists when law and politics are used by one economic
class to control and exploit another economic class. This definition
of the state was explicitly offered by Marx, Engels, and Lenin.[7]
The definitions of politics and law are not explicitly Marx's, but
I think can be used to elaborate the most valuable theses of *The
Civil War in France.* Accepting these definitions, then, it can be
shown that it is false to equate the state with politics and law
or to say they are necessary and sufficient conditions for each
other. For these arguments are based on the assumption that the

only purpose of law and politics is to keep the class system operating and that since socialism ends the class system, it also would end politics and law. But there is another purpose that politics and law would have in socialism—to keep the world economy operating. Furthermore, that this would require the existence of politics and law can be shown in the following way.

For Marx, the working class in socialism would consciously plan the distribution of labor and goods and the production of goods.[8] This is one way of differentiating socialism from capitalism where these functions are accomplished at least in part by the market. However, it seems reasonable that in order for this to occur there must be a system of rights, expectations, and obligations concerning people's role in this economy. This system of rights would not have to be and, indeed, was not meant to be hierarchical. But it would be difficult to make sure that society produced enough of the right kind of goods, if some people did not have the expectation and the obligation to perform work in some areas, others in other areas and if all people did not have the right to expect others to do their share. It is reasonable also that these moral obligations, rights, and duties should be stated in a publicly observable set of laws and that these laws should be used to facilitate agreement among men. Thus, even without the state there still would be a need for law and politics. It is only against this background that Marx's discussion in *The Civil War in France* can be understood.

The Civil War in France is a discussion of the Paris Commune. In 1871, in the midst of a war between Germany and France, the workers of Paris managed to liberate the city for a short time in a dual struggle against both Bismarck's troops and their own ruling class. This liberated city fell eventually to the government forces of Versailles. Since then the rapidly doomed liberation zone, called by its defenders the Paris Commune, has become a symbol of international working-class struggle. In addition, some of the features of the Commune have been carefully studied because of their foreshadowing of a Socialist society. Marx himself called the Commune the "political form at last discovered under which to work out the emancipation of labor."[9] This certainly does not mean that he saw its accomplishments as the achievements of a mature Socialist society. He couldn't have, since the Commune did not end the market and put the plan in its place. Nevertheless, in the besieged condition of the city there was a breakdown of some of the individualism of the market; its economy and affairs were run with a new political form which Marx carefully describes and commends.

Marx's discussion can conveniently be broken down into what he says about the Paris Commune and what he says about the potential relation that it would have had to the rest of France if the Communards had succeeded. The Communards had envisaged, and Marx praises them for this, that all of France would be divided into communes. The commune, then, would be a geographical unity having a certain political form. Furthermore, the relationship between the communes would entail a novel political form. Marx says of this relationship: "The unity of the nation was not to be broken, but, on the contrary, to be organized by the communal constitution."[10] It is clear from Marx's discussion of this centralized government that it also, like the commune itself, foreshadowed the political form of the emancipation of labor under socialism. For its central task was to connect the agricultural economy of the country to the industrial economy of the city. In doing this it would have used law and politics to bring about those allocations of labor and goods that must be planned in socialism. Marx is particularly careful to stress that the connection between the communes was not what the Anarchists imagined with their crucial claim that the emancipation of labor needs no centralization. Marx argues that there will be centralization, but that it will not be incompatible with democracy. Thus, the plan for the relation between the communes, if it is successful, answers one of the oldest charges that has been made against socialism—that socialism will give all power to a centralized government and that there will be no room left for the activity of the masses.

With these points in mind the actual democratic organization of the communal structure must be examined. Each commune would run the aspects of its own affairs that did not need to be integrated with the central body. Five points stand out in Marx's discussion: (1) Representatives to the communes would be elected by universal suffrage. (2) These representatives would be both legislative and executive. (3) They would be given specific instructions by the voters (the *mandat imperatif*) about which laws they should make and how they should act. (4) The representatives would be subject to recall. (5) The communal representatives would in turn elect representatives who would form a centralized body uniting the various communes.[11] These points are only sketched by Marx, and I now present my own analysis and defense of them. I will then connect that analysis with Colletti's account of the three cornerstones:

Representatives to the communes would be elected by universal suffrage. Since for Rousseau democracy in the strictest sense meant that the people themselves ran the government in all its aspects, this situation is incompatible with Rousseau's strict definition of democracy. Rousseau's looser definition of democracy, however, simply entails that the people make all the laws. But again this is not adhered to here, since the representatives make the laws, even though there are stringent controls on them by the people.

These representatives would be both legislative and executive. This seems to be what causes Marx's analysis to be less directly democratic than Rousseau's. However, it probably represents the fact that for Marx the laws have to do with the control of industrial production whereas for Rousseau they have to do with more traditional political tasks. The division of labor between the executive and legislative reflects an opposition between thought and action which Marx and the Communards perhaps did not think appropriate for the control of the economy. To use a homely example, it may be more practical for the person who is organizing a certain agricultural task to be able to formulate it and put it into practice at the same time. For Marx, then, the breaking down of the legislative and executive appears in the context of a theory of socialism where it refers to the control by the working class of the rules that regulate the economy. Thus, the central element that Marx has added to Rousseau here is that instead of a renewal of the social contract whenever the people either convene the legislative body or else become for a time more active in the executive body, the association of the people that make up the contract is constantly renewed and revitalized within the factories and the economic system. Marx no longer has to cling to the abstract moral injunction of achieving democracy through legislative activity. Now people must achieve democracy constantly in practice by controlling the economy instead of letting it control them.

Representatives would be given specific instructions by the voters about which laws they should make and how they should act. When these specific instructions are about how the representatives should act, this is very close to Rousseau's concept of the government as errand boy following the specific instructions of the people. The notion of specific instructions about how representatives should legislate, however, is a revision of Rousseau's claim that only the people should legislate.

It could be asked, however, if the representatives are told exactly what laws to make, then isn't this the same as the people making the laws? But if this is the case why don't they simply make the laws in the first place? Thus, if the *mandat imperatif* is taken literally it is useless since the people might as well make the laws in the first place; on the other hand, if it is efficacious, and if the mandated representatives serve a function, then legislative activity is taken farther away from the people. There are several possible answers to this objection that neither Colletti nor Marx explicitly make. The first is that the *mandat imperatif* must be thought of as a relative rather than as an absolute tightening of the will of the people to the lawmaking of the representatives. But the notion that this needs to be tightened suggests that it can be loosened. How is this possible? Isn't it the case that if people simply vote for the representatives, then the tie between representatives and people becomes as tight as it can be? The answer must be no and the question of the degree of tightness depends on a causal analysis of the creation of laws.

In some situations the primary cause of the laws made by representatives might be the knowledge that the people who elected them want a certain type of law. In some situations the primary cause of the law made by representatives may be interest in serving another purpose entirely than that of the people who elected them. Certainly anyone would admit that this is logically

possible and factually true of certain situations. The only disagreement is over how often it is factually true. Anyone would
have to admit today that it was true for the Watergate government.
Marx, however, noted in *The Civil War in France* that it was true
of American and indeed capitalist politics in general that those
who are elected do not serve the interests of those who elect them
but rather of the wealthy. Of course, there will be wide disagreements over this factual analysis, but it seems that the conceptual
analysis of the *mandat imperatif* can be independent of it, and
simply ask the question of how to create a situation where the
laws passed by the legislator are primarily caused by the will of
the people who elected that legislator.

Several other questions need to be analyzed. First, how is
this tightening possible without reverting to a situation where all
the people make the laws? Second, is the same amount of tightening always desirable? Third, are there objections to be made
against such a tightening?

To answer the problem of how to tie the legislator tightly to
the people's will without making the people legislators, we must
assume that the representatives will sometimes be able to act without the explicit approval of the people. Thus, the legislator would
be judged in terms of his general responsiveness to the ideas that
the electorate will have asked him to follow. Sometimes he may
have to act on a specific application of those ideas, without their
instructions. But afterwards he will again check with them to at
least get their retroactive agreement. If the representative did not
attempt to get this feedback often enough or if he was unskillful
in moving from the general to the particular, then this would be
a possible cause for recall. It might be objected that in a large
state such constant feedback between the representatives and the
people would be difficult. However, modern informational tech-
niques may be a way of avoiding Rousseau's scepticism about
the possibility of mass participation in a large country. It might
be possible, for example, to have some of the information that
the representative gets from the people and vice versa exchanged
via computers.

The second problem raised was whether it would be desirable
to always have the same amount of tightness between the ideas

of the people and the executive and legislative activity of the representative. The answer would seem to be no. This would depend
on the technical and moral importance of the questions being debated. It seems that a Socialist society would only be possible if
it was assumed, as in some ethical systems, that good moral principles are universal. Some of the questions in the Socialist society
would revolve directly around the application of these moral
principles to specific examples whereas some would be questions
of skill and judgment. What I have in mind by the difference
between these three, moral principles, application, and skill, may
be indicated by the following example. A moral principle may
be that each person should get what he needs. Then a particular
application of that moral principle would be whether this family
needs more than that. Then a question of skill arising out of this
would be how to give the one family more than the other. For
the communal system to work it has to be assumed that the basic
principle was held by both electorate and representative. Its
application to the family and the carrying out of the principle
would have to be analyzed by both together; but presumably the
representative could be given more leeway in the question of skill
than in the direct application of the moral principle to the concrete problem of determining which family needs more.

The third problem had to do with whether it is always desirable to have an extremely tight connection between the people's
will and the action of the representative. It has been argued by
John Stuart Mill, for example, that the representative should be
free for long periods of time to act according to his own conscience.[12] However, it seems that Mill simply is emphasizing one
of the two aspects of democracy that Rousseau and Marx stress—
the idea that there must be correct principles and that sometimes
only a few will have those principles. Socialist democracy, in the
sense that we are discussing it, however, must make its rules
according to the assumption that the majority are committed to
equality and that there is the opportunity for all people to enter
fully into the political process. The assumption is that this optimum situation exists and the problem then is how to technically
work out the interaction between centralization and localization.
Mill and others who defend the autonomy of the representative

are not assuming that that optimum situation exists. Indeed, they are not even operating in the conceptual framework that allows that optimum situation to be sketched. Some of the differences between my position and Mill's position might be obviated if this is taken into consideration. On my position the representative should not in general be left on his own conscience. Insofar as he is left alone, it will be rather on his own skill. However, this assumes that the masses of people have genuinely adopted the principles of equality and the willingness to participate fully in the democratic process that goes along with this. If that optimum situation is not yet realized then I might agree with Mill in certain concrete cases. A representatitive in a country carrying on even a popularly supported imperialist war should go against the will of those who elected him. Indeed, if he has a chance he should do everything possible to follow his own moral principles rather than the ones that they have explicitly given him. However, to comprehend this it is necessary to bring out two points that Mill neglects. First, on my analysis, the possibility of the moral vanguardism of the representative is only that—a possibility. Mill seems to think that it is a necessity. It is also possible, insofar as socialism is possible, that this moral vanguardism will end. Second, representatives do not grow out of an economic vacuum. Either they are connected with a political system that generates and continues economic inequalities or they are not. If the former, then it is highly doubtful that very many representatives, even if they do not follow the will of the people who represent them, will be able to avoid serving the will of those whose interests it is to see that the system of economic inequalities persists. For it is not the case that just because the representative does not follow the will of the electorate, therefore he automatically follows his own will. On the other hand, if the representative is not part of a system of inequalities, then there is no reason for moral vanguardism.

The representatives would be subject to recall. This condition is conceptually connected with the *mandat imperatif* and simply gives it teeth. It makes no sense to say that the representative must follow the will of the people if there is no way of insuring that he does so. Recall allows such insurance.

The communal representatives would in turn elect representatives who would form a centralized body uniting the various communes. The details of this plan are not worked out in Marx's discussion or in the original notes of the Communards. Probably it is best to imagine it visually as having a pyramidal structure. At the bottom there are the various communes, each commune taking care of its business. Then, overarching this basis, is a centralized communal decision-making body which is elected by the various representatives from the communes. Both sets of representatives perform both executive and legislative tasks. However, this sketch does not really show how the communal structure is to fulfill the assigned task of preventing a bureaucratic centralized power. To see its potential for doing this more features must be sketched.

The visual pyramid must become more intricate. First, it is obvious that there can be a whole series of intermediate bodies between the communes at the bottom and the central body at the top. The purpose of multiplying these bodies would be to break down the opposition between political power and everyday life, not arbitrarily but in the direction in which it would be easiest and most worthwhile to do so. There may be fifty communes at the bottom. These might be divided into five groups of ten each. These groups could in turn elect representatives. These five sets of representatives could then meet at the highest body.

But this quantitative expansion of intermediate bodies would be worthless if it were not supplemented with a carefully thought-out method of how to divide the quantitative elements. It is not obvious, for example, that the best method would be simply geographical. Indeed, it might be better to break up the communes in terms of the type of work that they are doing and in terms of their potential role in the division of labor. For it is the division of labor and distribution of goods that would be the central task of the commune anyway. However, the exact form that these quantitative and qualitative divisions would take could only be decided in socialism itself. Indeed, much of the energy which in pre-Socialist society goes into the study of law and economics could be profitably devoted to solving these problems.

The notions that we have just been discussing place Marx on a somewhat different political terrain than Rousseau. Rousseau had shied away from any plans for dividing the people up. Instead he had always stressed the importance of a unified people. Rousseau took this stand against those thinkers who thought of the state as an arbitrator between various groups of unequal and divided people. As opposed to this, Rousseau stressed that the people must be unified and for him. This entailed a considerable uniformity in wealth and possessions.

However, it is not obvious that the separation of people into communes entails acceptance of social equality. Rather for this type of decentralization to work, there must first be created a common ground upon which people can meet. This common ground is found in the concept of equal control of industrial production, a concept which blends Rousseau's emphasis on the moral commitment aspect of democracy with Marx's stress on how that moral commitment applies to the concrete problems of controlling the economy. It is because people share these common goals that the economy can be as decentralized as Marx imagines it.

This can be elaborated in the following way. For Rousseau there was a problem of bringing together commitment to basic moral principles, such as equality, with mass action. One way of trying to resolve this problem is to debate within a given situation about how it can best be approached. Should I now trust the masses? Should I now trust my principles? However, another way is to try to bring about a situation where the optimum of both can be achieved. One way of approaching this would be to create a situation where people have similar enough interests so that they could more easily apply basic moral principles to those interests. In capitalism it oftentimes seems to people that they do not have such similar interests because they appear to each other as competitors. But when people come to grips with the common necessity of distributing labor and goods for the good of the whole, without first having to produce as private property owners, then the common interests and hopefully the common moral principles will come to the fore. However, the ideal of common moral interests is not one which is imposed on people but one which they constantly look at afresh from the standpoint of both their individual and social activity. Local autonomy, then, on the part of workers, does not mean that they will decide against the interest of the whole. Rather, it may help them come to grips freely with their own social nature.

This is the type of optimum situation aimed at by the communal structure. Thus, the commune aims at solving the paradox of democracy—that the moral principles of equality may be divorced from mass action. The theoretical solution to the problem of democracy is to find a situation where the movement of masses of individuals is in conformity with the principles of equality, principles which are supra-individual. Similarly, the optimum situation aimed at in the commune is to create an economy which, because it appeals to the basic common interests of people, allows them to be truly themselves at the same time that they are truly working for the common good.

How about Colletti's cornerstones of democracy? It is obvious that they capture a significant aspect of the commune. For, first, the commune certainly involves a critique of the parliamentary representative state. Second, it stresses the recall of delegates, and third, it stresses the ultimate disappearance of the state. In regard to the first, however, I have suggested that some, but only some, aspects of the old parliamentary politics will still be used in the commune and in society in general. In regard to the second, I have shown that Marx admits, as opposed to Rousseau, that legislative representatives can be elected without destroying democracy. Finally, in analyzing the third, I have emphasized that the state can be abolished without returning to a situation where all features of political life have been abolished. I have argued that getting rid of the state does not mean getting rid of law.

Colletti also locates another line of pre-Socialist Democratic theory, one which is identified most prominently with Locke.[13] The major difference between Locke and Rousseau strikes us as soon as we confront the first condition for democracy—the refusal to accept elected lawmakers. For Locke, unlike Rousseau, accepts such elected representative legislative bodies and Colletti argues that this reflects a deep schism in their views of the theory of social contract. One aspect of this theory locates the origin of political society in a series of promises or a contract that people make.

Whereas, for Locke, there is a contract between the people and the ruler, the government; for Rousseau the only contract is among the people who make up the legislative body. It is the Lockian view of the contract that leads to the concept of political democracy and equality coming only through the state. This is connected with its stress on the importance of parliament as a group separated from the people and on the separation of powers in the state, a view which holds that equality is guaranteed, not by the activity of the people, but by the competition for power among those who control the state. Rousseau, on the other hand, by stressing that the contract is among the people and not between the people and the ruler, is able to show that the government is not separated from the people and that equality is not given to them by the state, but rather something that they must take for themselves.

Several other points can be used to supplement Colletti's general observations about the contrast between Locke and Rousseau. One has to do with revolution. It could be argued that Locke is the theoretician of revolution rather than Rousseau. A significant portion of the *Second Treatise of Government* is concerned with justifying revolutions under certain conditions, whereas *The Social Contract* hardly ever deals with this as a specific topic. But this point can be turned upside down. Why does Locke spend so much time justifying revolution under specific conditions? Because ordinarily there is nothing like a revolution going on at all. The state is simply ruling in the interests of at least some of the people who accept these benefits passively. They may revolt if they are not getting their benefits. But they revolt simply to return again to their old passivity. Rousseau, on the other hand, does not overly concern himself with any specific right to revolution, because he regards democracy itself as a permanent revolution against inequalities and against those who want to rule without being directly accountable to the people.

A second point has to do with property. There is an obvious connection between Rousseau's notion of the contract among the people and his relatively egalitarian attitudes toward property. He seems to have moved from the notion of the people's commitment to equality, brought about by their contract with themselves, to the notion that they all, as members of the legislative body, have equal control over property, even though in practice they may allow some people to use more property than others. Locke on the other hand, does not see the contract in terms of the people committing themselves to equality and, consequently, does not make any moves toward an egalitarian theory of property within the political state. This suggests that there is an inner connection between questions of democracy and questions about the extent and nature of socialization of property.[14]

The cleavages between the two theories of democracy are ultimately used by Colletti to analyze the difference between various attitudes toward socialism in the late nineteenth and twentieth centuries, primarily German social democracy, Leninism, and Stalinism.

Colletti argues that the German Social Democrats of the late nineteenth and early twentieth centuries gradually began to interpret Marx in the light of the Lockian theory of the state, so that for them democracy and socialism itself are given to people by the state.[15] Colletti argues that this reasoning underlies the decision of the Social Democrats to concentrate almost exclusively upon electing Socialists to the parliament. The implications of this reasoning, he argues, are as follows. The German Social Democrats had come to hold that the primary inconsistency in modern capitalist societies was between political equality and economic inequality. They thought that Socialists should use the political equality which they thought was already granted by the capitalist state to elect representatives who then would create conditions of economic equality. What they did not see was that the political equality that they had was based upon the separation of the state from the people. This is Locke's state-guaranteed equality, not Rousseau's active achievement of equality. It can further be argued that a socialism which was based upon the equality that is given to the people by the state can never attain the conception of mass rule by the people but will conceive of socialism itself as a system where the state distributes goods to its passive citizens. Colletti says of this tendency in German social democracy that "the rise to power of particular political personnel, rather than a modification of the roots on which the power structure rests, is seen as decisive for socialism."[16] The Social Democrats began to think that the existing state should simply be used to achieve socialism. Thus it spurned the democratic heritage of Rousseau and, if Colletti is right, of Marx. But in spurning this democratic heritage it also spurned the revolutionary heritage of Marxism. The existing state is not something to be struggled against, but something to be worked within.

Colletti's analysis of these flaws in German social democracy is supplemented by his analysis of Lenin's achievement of a revolutionary democratic theory in *The State and Revolution*. Colletti argues that the cornerstones of democracy appear again in this book. His task of showing this is made easier by the fact that a crucial part of the argument of *State and Revolution* is based on Lenin's interpretation of *The Civil War in France*. Lenin follows both Rousseau and Marx in (1) criticizing the representative state, (2) his stress on revocable delegates, and (3) his idea of the necessity of revolting against the old state apparatus. Thus, Lenin's stress on democracy is connected with his stress on revolution. This revolution, however, is not simply violent acts but the attempt on the part of the proletariat to directly control their own lives:

Here we have the really basic theme of *State and Revolution*. The destruction of the bourgeois state machine is not the ministry of the interior in flames, it is not the barricades. All this may take place, but it is not the essential point. What is essential to the revolution is the destruction of the diaphragm that separates the working classes from power, the emancipation and self-determination of the former, the transmission of power into the hands of the people. Marx said that the Commune had proved that "the working class cannot simply lay hold of the ready-made state machinery and wield it for its own purposes." It cannot; for the aim of the socialist revolution is not to "transfer the bureaucratic-military machine from one hand to another" but to transfer power directly into the hands of the people—and that is impossible if this machine is not first smashed.[17]

Finally, Colletti presents an analysis of Stalinism. As opposed to social democracy, which sees the concept of political equality as something positive and attained by the representative state, and Leninism, which sees political equality as something positive but limited and not even attained by the representative state, there is another current of thought and practice in communism and socialism which "considers political equality as a mere trap."[18] This is one aspect of Stalinism. Stalinism holds that since the Socialist revolution will abolish the organs of the representative state it will also abolish institutions connected with the representative state, such as freedom of the press, free elections, and the right to strike.[19]

Stalinism, for Colletti, also has another side which is content to liberate itself through the modern representative state. Viewed from this angle it appears identical with social democracy. Is Colletti confused and has he given two contradictory definitions of Stalinism? Rather this oscillation characterizes Stalinism and it is clear that insofar as a broader definition of Stalinism can be found in the writings of Colletti, Stalinism in the largest sense includes both social democracy, the moment of optimism about the representative state and the moment of the negative attitude toward all forms of political equality, especially those associated with the representative state.

Colletti has supplied the key to this definition in an article on Gramsci and his attitude toward the sixth and seventh congresses of the Third (Stalinist) International.[20] The sixth and seventh congresses, held respectively in 1928 and 1935, recommended two very different methods of fighting fascism. The sixth argued that the Communist parties should make no allowances of any kind with those who would defend the democratic representative state against fascism, one of whose features is the ending of the democratic representative state, not to surpass it in terms of the struggle for equality but rather to go beneath it. This policy was singularly unsuccessful and led to the seventh congress resolving upon an entirely different course. Far from not allying with those who defend the democratic representative state against fascism, Communists should place the preservation of that state at the top of their list of priorities, the famous Popular Front strategy. Gramsci's thought, Colletti argues, is opposed to the views of both congresses. Against the former, he had argued that in a country like Italy with its small proletariat the Communists should aim at allying with the peasants and the petty bourgeoisie and, in doing this, raise the slogan of a constituent assembly, i.e., a democratic representative state. This was his argument against the view of the sixth congress. However, Gramsci had not thought that the Communist party should stop with this demand, but rather that it should demonstrate to the Italian working class that the "only solution possible in Italy is the proletarian revolution."[21] Thus, for Colletti, Gramsci's thought is inconsistent with the resolution of the seventh congress. Colletti's aim, then, is to show Gramsci's stand against the double face of Stalinism, both when it remains at the level of the democratic representative state and when it falls behind it. For us, its importance lies in this clear analysis of that very double face. What, however, are the roots of this double face of Stalinism? Colletti partially answers this through an analysis of the early period of the Russian revolution.[22]

Those who made the Russian revolution were forced to do so before capitalism was fully achieved; thus before the majority, or even a large minority, of the people were members of the proletariat. Such a revolution, when considered by itself, lacked both the industrial basis and the majoritarian basis to create socialism. For Colletti there cannot be socialism without that potential for ending scarcity that is given by modern industry. He notes that Lenin and Trotsky were aware of these deficiencies and stressed that they could only be remedied if the advanced Western world pitched in to help by having its own revolution. The Socialist revolution must be international. International support would have allowed the Soviets to pre-industrialize rapidly—and thus overcome general scarcity—and to become a free and open Socialist society permeated by democratic processes. The West, however, did not pitch in, and Russia, guided by Stalin, became preoccupied with nationalist goals and unconcerned with building revolution in the world outside or achieving democratic socialism within.

This account needs to be extended in an effort to explain and identify other manifestations of the social democratic or Stalinist paths. Colletti's efforts at such further identification and explanation seem to lead him, however, in the direction of generally condemning any Socialist group which uses political forms to achieve socialism. This attitude is undoubtedly based on his tendency to interpret the disappearance of the state as the negation of politics and law rather than as their transformation.

This tendency was first revealed in Colletti's analysis of *The Critique of Hegel's Doctrine of the State,* where he tended to blur the differences between Rousseau's theory of democracy and law and Marx's somewhat Feuerbachian account of Communist man expressing his human nature outside of social institutions. As opposed to this, my interpretation of the *Critique* stressed the peculiarities of the nineteenth-century German philosophical milieu in which it was written. I argued that the German philosophers, including Marx, were discussing the issue of commitment to ethical principles, but that other, more political, aspects of Rousseau's discussion of democracy were often lacking. Thus, in Marx's *Critique* he tends to interpret the disappearance of the state as simply the negation of law and politics. On the other hand, I argued that in *The Civil War in France* he applies law and politics to the running of the economy, after the state, the institution by which one class oppresses another, has disappeared. I do not want to overstress this difference between Colletti and myself, for I agree with his general opposition between the Rousseauian and the Lockian theories of democracy. I further agree with his use of it to analyze Lenin's original vision of the Russian revolution, the activity of the German Social Democrats, and Stalinism, both in its Russian version and in the frontism which Stalinism imposed on the Third International. However, once we moved beyond these paradigmatic cases, then my legal and political interpretation of the commune would undoubtedly sometimes lead in a different direction from Colletti on the issue of identification and explanation of what exactly counts for Stalinism, or social democracy, or the practical application of the Rousseau-Marx-Lenin theory of democracy.

In conclusion, Colletti has shown the good of democratic socialism as opposed to German social democracy and Stalinism. He has not, however, always delved adequately into the concrete conditions that would allow the former, rather than the latter, to be actualized. But as Colletti himself points out in a 1974 interview, the renewal of revolutionary democratic socialism requires practice as well as theory.[23] Such a renewed practice would also, as Colletti suggests, give rise to new and more concrete theoretical works. Such theory and practice will hopefully have learned from Colletti and the general discussion of socialism and democracy in Italy. One of its main tasks will be to show in detail how working people can achieve new types of democratic self-rule as they come to control the economy. Since this Socialist economy will be new, the types of democratic self-rule will also be new. Socialism is more than the improved production and distribution of goods. It is also the production of the basis for the most complete self-rule possible.

Bibliography

Colletti, Lucio. *From Rousseau to Lenin*. New York: Monthly Review, 1972.

Colletti, Lucio. *Marxism and Hegel*. London: New Left Books, 1973.

Colletti, Lucio. "The Question of Stalin," *New Left Review*, no. 61, May-June, 1970.

Colletti, Lucio. "Gramsci and Revolution," *New Left Review*, no. 65, January-February, 1971.

Colletti, Lucio. "Marx, Hegel e la scuola di Francoforte," *Riniscita*, May 14, 1971.

Colletti, Lucio. "A Political and Philosophical Interview," *New Left Review*, no. 86, July-August, 1974.

Colletti, Lucio. "Contradiction and Contrariety," *New Left Review*, no. 93, September-October, 1975.

Colletti, Lucio, ed. *Karl Marx, Early Writings*. New York: Vintage, 1975. (Contains Marx's *Critique of Hegel's Doctrine of the State*.)

Della Volpe, Galvano. "Marx and Rousseau," *New Left Review*, no. 59, January-February, 1970.

Gramsci, Antonio. *Selections from the Prison Notebooks*. New York: International Publishers, 1971.

Lenin, V. I. *The State and Revolution*. Peking: Foreign Languages Press, 1965.

Locke, John. *Two Treatises of Government*. New York: New American Library, 1965. (This includes *The Second Treatise of Government*.)

Macciocchi, Maria-Antonietta. *Pour Gramsci*. Paris: Éditions de Seuil, 1974.

Magri, Lucio. "Italian Communism Today." *New Left Review*, no. 66, March-April, 1971.

Marx, Karl. *The First International and After*. New York: Vintage, 1974. (This includes *The Civil War in France*.)

Rousseau, Jean-Jacques. *The Social Contract*. New York: Hafner, 1947.

Chapter 5

Socialism and
Individual
Freedom

Humanistic Socialism: Erich Fromm
by Theodore Bickley

The following selection deals primarily with Eric Fromm's theory of the nature of the self and his theory of value. An effort is made to see how his view of the self and value serve to lead him in the direction of a Socialist humanism. The Socialist humanism that Fromm espouses is non-authoritarian in character and represents an emphasis on a social structure which is consistent with personal freedom and individual fulfillment. While he holds that the social order should be structured so as to protect against the exploitation of individuals by other individuals and institutions, the social order in turn must not itself become a repressive instrument in which the freedom and fulfillment of the individual is denied.

How can I find fulfillment through the development of my own autonomy and at the same time be a responsible "social" being who must live in a world where other human beings live, too? In attempting to solve this problem, the philosophical pendulum often swings from the one extreme to the other.

On the one hand, it is announced that self-fulfillment can take place only with the sacrifice of self in some "grander" whole (as in theories of the social order in which "individualism" is considered reactionary and out-of-date). Totalitarian schemes, whether of left or right, have often seen individual persons as expendable in the attainment of some larger social purpose.

On the other hand, the philosophical pendulum has, in reaction to what it claims is the loss of genuine selfhood and the depersonalization resulting from totalitarian schemes, moved in the opposite direction which is best expressed in modern-day existentialism. In the existentialist reaction to "system" (whether in metaphysics or anywhere else), the stress has been to emphasize again the importance of the individual and his or her life, the uniqueness of individual value and meaning and the recapturing of what the existentialists call "authentic living" and "authentic selfhood." Such "authenticity" is usually defined in terms of the development of one's own autonomy and one's own life-style.

Again, however, in reaction to such individualistic emphasis, the philosophical pendulum may swing in an anti-individualistic direction as conflicts emerge between individuals. At such times it is charged that we have lost a "social" principle or that the social principle was too drastically and radically sacrificed to the importance of individual meaning and autonomy. For example, if I pursue my own aims, needs, goals, and meanings, and this moves me into conflict with someone else's goals, meanings, aims, and so forth, a problem arises. The problem is: How do I reconcile the establishment and fulfillment of my own life and meanings with a possible conflict with other lives who presumably are following their own drive toward authenticity also?

To return, then, to our original problem: In the process of my being *me,* what kind of philosophy is it which can keep me from denying you your right to be *you*? To be sure, "doing one's own thing" does not mean that conflict with others "doing their thing" is inevitable. Yet, the social conflict clearly indicates that more analysis is needed than simply asserting everyone should be able to do their own thing. Some things that are your own thing may not have the social consequences which some other things may have. For example, doing my own thing may be appreciating a beautiful sunset. But the social consequences of appreciating a beautiful sunset are far different from someone who declares that doing his or her "own thing" means robbing a bank.

Where does all this lead us? First, it seems clear that we must protect ourselves against loss from both directions. If human persons become computerized robots or are socially programmed so much that the meaning of freedom and authenticity is watered down to nothing such that we are afraid to even assert or argue our case, it would have to be admitted that something serious has happened to the human person. On the other hand, if my individualism becomes pure exploitation of others and I see myself as the center of the universe who has some universal right to treat other persons always as "means" to my ends and never as "ends" in themselves, an equally severe problem looms.

Erich Fromm struggles with the aforementioned problem in a unique way. The uniqueness lies, as I see it, in his effort to always keep his eye on the individual as well as the social.

We need to note also that Fromm's philosophy is humanistic in orientation. His analysis of the self and his theory of value combine to persuade him that a Socialist order of society built on humanist foundations will best serve human need. The Socialist humanism which he espouses is nonauthoritarian in character and represents an emphasis on a social structure which is consistent with personal freedom and individual fulfillment. While he holds that the social order should be structured so as to protect against the exploitation of individuals by other individuals, the social order in turn must not itself become a repressive instrument in which the freedom and fulfillment of the individual is denied. We try to see how his view of the self and value lead him in the direction of a Socialist-type of humanism.

We proceed with Fromm's analysis. We deal with two aspects of his thesis. We treat first his philosophy of the nature of selfhood. Second, we interpret his theory of value.

We begin with what Fromm holds to be two basic factors about human nature. Let us note first what Fromm thinks human nature is not. Human nature is not in his view simply a biologically fixed and sum total of drives, although "the necessity to satisfy the physiologically conditioned drives"[1] is fixed and unchangeable. Likewise, human nature is not a mere lifeless shadow of cultural and social patterns to which it "adapts itself smoothly." In other words, our nature as a person is not a mere social product. The implication of this position that we are not merely biological-social products is of considerable consequence in my view and we will need to pursue this matter later.

Yet, while we are not a mere product of our culture, that which is fixed and unchangeable here is, says Fromm, "the necessity to avoid isolation and moral aloneness."[2]

Fromm sees human development as a thrust toward autonomy and independence. The self, then, emerges in a kind of two-fold situation. On the one hand, its security is based on the necessary fulfillment of its physiologically determined needs along with the necessity of satisfying the need for "belonging"; on the other hand, as the individual self develops there is an increasing thrust toward freedom and independence.

The movement toward individuation must be seen in the light of what Fromm calls the "primary ties." These primary ties (child with mother, primitive community with clan, medieval man with church and social caste) are like an umbilical cord which fastens him to the world outside himself. According to Fromm, this means heteronomy and lack of freedom. But the irony is that the same conditions which create heteronomy and lack of freedom provide at the same time feelings of security and belonging, of being rooted somewhere.

As individuality develops and the individual begins to realize more autonomy and freedom, these primary ties begin to weaken. As those ties weaken, a threat is posed with respect to the earlier security and belongingness which was provided by these early primary ties. In other words, says Fromm, one needs "to orient and root himself in the world and to find security in other ways than those which were characteristic of his preindividual existence."[3]

To this point, then, Fromm seems to be asking: In the light of the breaking of the umbilical cords, how do I relate myself to the world so that I can again find security in belonging without at the same time sacrificing my individuality? We pursue the matter further.

One side of the process of individuation is what Fromm calls the growth of "self-strength." But as the process of individuation increases a loss of a sense of unity with the outside world takes place. The primary ties offered unity and basic security. The process of individuation becomes a process of growing "aloneness."

The emerging problem, then, has to do with the issue of relating one's self to the outside world. Fromm believes that a positive relationship can be reestablished (through love and productive work) in which the individual connects himself with the world without eliminating his individuality. But there is also the danger that he will sacrifice his individuality in terms of a submission in order to regain a sense of security. When this happens his relationship to the outside world becomes a "mechanism of escape" or, better, a submerging of his individuality rather than a fulfillment of it.

There is, then, in Fromm's view a dialectical character to the emerging of individuality through freedom. On the one hand, our freedom and autonomy can, through love and productive work, relate us positively to the world and other persons. On the other hand, the assertion of our freedom can also lead toward increasing isolation and insecurity causing "growing doubt concerning one's role in the universe, the meaning of one's life, and with all that a growing feeling of one's own powerlessness and insignificance as an individual."[4]

Fromm holds that from the Reformation onward the "aloneness" and "isolation" of the individual has been accentuated rather than resolved; that is, the religious and economic conditions have been such as to discourage rather than encourage the positive reuniting of the human being with his world.

Once the primary ties are cut and the individual begins to experience him or her self as a separate entity, the human being (having lost the earlier securities) has to overcome the powerlessness and aloneness which threatens. How the newfound freedom is handled becomes a crucial issue to Fromm.

One can progress to what Fromm calls "positive freedom":

> . . . he can relate himself spontaneously to the world in love and work, in the genuine expression of his emotional, sensuous, and intellectual capacities; he can thus become one again with man, nature and himself without giving up the independence and integrity of his individual self.[5]

The other route in the handling of the freedom is essentially to give it up in order to eliminate the gap that arose between self and world with his emerging autonomy and individuality. For example, one turns over to the society, state, or social order the freedom to be one's self independent of the social plan, and receives in return the promise of a secure existence, the sense of belonging to something wider than oneself, and so forth. The giving up of freedom in order to reestablish some unity does not really work, however, because we always remain individuals and the separateness cannot be reversed. The giving up of the freedom has, says Fromm, a compulsive character to it (as when we are escaping from threatening panic) and consequently is a "surrender of individuality and the integrity of the self."[6]

To this point, the problem essentially for Fromm is: How do I preserve the autonomy and freedom (and thus the integrity of the self) consequent upon the development of individualization and yet use that freedom in ways which relate me in some positive way to the world?

We analyze in more detail the characteristics of the self which, in Fromm's view, contribute toward a positive reuniting of the self with the world. Before that reunification can occur, however, we need to begin with an analysis of the self; specifically, with what we would call a proper self-image. Fromm argues that the building of the self-image is a prerequisite to the reunification of self and world.

We may begin by noting Fromm's contention that religion, and specifically Protestantism, degraded love for oneself. He agrees, naturally, that there are wrong ways to love oneself but he does maintain that a proper regard and love for oneself is essential to a reuniting of man with himself which also becomes the building block for the reunification with the world.

The spiritual and economic individualism since the Protestant Reformation has not been, in Fromm's view, a healthy individualism. It has actually fostered the "aloneness" of human beings. Fromm holds that the submission of oneself to extrahuman ends was prepared by Protestantism specifically in the supremacy of economic activities although Luther and Calvin did not intend this. But, says Fromm, "in their theological teaching they had laid the ground for this development by breaking man's spiritual backbone, his feeling of dignity and pride, by teaching him that activity had no further aims outside himself."[7] In his isolation, man faces superior powers, for example, God, competitors, impersonal economic forces. This individualism was a strange variety. While on the one hand it stressed individual value, work, and initiative, it actually negated the worth and dignity of the individual, thus alienating the individual not only from himself but from his world as well.

We need to review in more depth how Fromm sees the conception we have of ourselves as setting the stage for the way we relate not only to ourselves but to the world around us.

Fromm does not equate selfishness with self-love. One must be able to affirm one's own life as well as that of others. Thus he says that if one can only "love others," he cannot love at all. Fromm sees selfishness as rooted in the lack of fondness for oneself. A genuine fondness and affirmation toward myself creates an inner security which is not present when we are abnormally concerned about ourselves. For example, the reason I want to get everything for myself is that I lack a basic security and satisfaction.

Thus, while from the service standpoint, it looks as though the selfish person "loves" himself, the fact is that he is actually not fond of himself at all since "selfishness" is really an overcompensation for lack of self-love.

This lack of proper self-love and self-affirmation (producing thereby a lack of inner security) often leads us to find the security we lack in ourselves in something outside ourselves in order to acquire the strength which the individual self is lacking. Submission or domination would be examples of this trend.

We may seek, for example, to become a part of a bigger or more powerful whole outside of ourselves, to submerge or participate in something bigger than ourselves as an avenue of escape from our own loneliness and powerlessness. "This power," says Fromm, "can be a person, an institution, God, nation, conscience, or a psychic compulsion."[8]

Both sadism and masochism are examples of this effort to escape from really being oneself. Fromm uses the term symbiosis to describe this effort at flight from oneself. By symbiosis he means the union of one individual self with another self (or any other power outside oneself). This union occurs in such a way "as to make each lose the integrity of its own self and to make them completely dependent on each other."[9] The masochist finds his security in being swallowed up by something else; the sadist, by swallowing up somebody else.

The frustrated and "unlived" self, the self which is not able to truly be itself, often may lash out in destructiveness. Fromm holds that life has a kind of inner dynamism; that is, it tends toward growth, seeks to be expressed and lived. When this tendency is blocked he believes that the unresolved energy undergoes a process of decomposition and finally emerges in destructive tendencies.[10]

In other words, both the drive for life and the drive for destruction are mutually related. When life is thwarted and blocked from fulfillment, the stronger the drive for destruction becomes. As Fromm puts it:

> Destructiveness is the outcome of unlived life. Those individual and social conditions that make for suppression of life produce the passion for destruction that forms, so to speak, the reservoir from which the particular hostile tendencies—either against others or against oneself—are nourished.[11]

When the self is suppressed or blocked from reaching its own identity and fulfillment, the aloneness once again catapults the self into seeking its identity through conformity to social patterns. By seeking a heteronomous identity, such a self is never really itself or ceases to be itself. The personality it adopts is offered to it by cultural patterns. Such a self escapes from its powerlessness and aloneness by becoming what others expect it to be. I become, for example, simply a reflection of those around me or simply a reflection of the socitey in which I live. I am my society. Thus, I escape my aloneness and the responsibility of being *me*.

The effort to conform is what Fromm calls a "pseudoself." The original self is replaced. In my view, Fromm is never clear enough on the factors constituting this "original" self. Be that as it may, the pseudoself is not the originator of its own mental activity. Not only does the pseudoself become an agent replacing the original self and representing itself in terms of a role, but the pseudoself comes to be thought of as the original self. The loss of the real and true self and its replacement by a pseudoself leaves the individual in a state of intense anxiety. The anxiety is due to the fact that one is not at one with his or her true self and because of this one is plagued with doubt about oneself primarily because the identity is a dependent identity; that is, the identity is essentially a reflection of other persons' expectations. The crucial point Fromm makes here, however, is that the self seeks to overcome its own lack of identity by being compelled to conform, to seek his identity by continuous approval and recognition by others.[12]

Fromm sees the Freudian idea of free association as a method to try to uncover the original self. Thus, free association is the free expression of one's original feelings and thoughts in such a way that the thinking itself is original and not "an adaptation to an expected thought."[13] A pseudoself would be a self expressing itself in terms of what it was *expected* to express. Its identity is therefore heteronomously determined.

We must note that Fromm differs from Freud in the interpretation of the foundations or origins of human nature. Fromm's position argues for an historically conditioned human nature. While he does not minimize the significance of biological factors, he nevertheless does not hold that human nature is just a matter of biological versus cultural factors. Freud saw human nature as biologically determined by certain physiological drives. The character development was in Freud's view a reaction to drive satisfaction or frustration. Fromm, on the other hand, says that his fundamental approach to human personality is that of understanding man's relation to the world, to others, to nature, and to himself. He writes: "We believe man is primarily a social being, and not, as Freud assumes, primarily self-sufficient and only secondarily in need of others in order to satisfy instinctual needs."[14]

This stress on the relation between man's individual selfhood and his social existence, the interpenetration of the one with the other, is the crux of Fromm's thesis. It is impossible for us to understand either the individual or social end of our existence without understanding the relating character of human personality, the relating to one's own self, to others, to nature, and to the world. It shall be our purpose next to see how that relating process is central to the development of human character in Fromm's thought and how his theory of value and his humanistic ethics grow out of the relating thesis.

Fromm is arguing that the integrity of the self is dependent on a respect for, and development of, freedom and personal fulfillment. A healthy self-image of one's worth and value is necessary not only in establishing a degree of inner psychological security (thus protecting against escapist ventures for security) but it provides the basis for a constructive and positive relating to others. Frustration and blockage of the thrust toward freedom and personal fulfillment alienates us both from ourselves and others. In other words, healthy socialization is impossible without the positive contribution of a healthy self-love. We turn now to his theory of value.

Fromm speaks of his theory of value as a humanistically oriented ethic. He wrote *Man for Himself* with the intention of reaffirming the validity of humanistic ethics, "to show that our knowledge of human nature does not lead to ethical relativism but, on the contrary, to the conviction that the sources of norms for ethical conduct are to be found in man's nature itself. . . ."[15]

The necessity of a healthy self-love is carried forward in his theory of value through his view that the character structure of the mature and integrated personality is what he calls a "productive" character. The good for Fromm lies in the direction of the productive character while "vice" is actually an indifference to oneself or even a self-mutilation. "Not self-renunciation nor selfishness," says Fromm, "but self-love, not the negation of the individual but the affirmation of his truly human self, are the supreme values of humanistic ethics."[16]

"Character" is the term Fromm uses to indicate the nature of an individual's orientation to the world. He defines character as a relatively permanent form in which human energy " is canalized in the process of assimilation and socialization."[17]

We noted earlier how freedom of the self was a unique characteristic of the self, that is, the development of autonomous action. This unique capacity, when we relate it to human evolution, means that the story of human evolution is a story of man's ability at adapting himself. For Fromm, human nature is not simply a blank sheet of paper upon which culture writes. Human nature has its own specific ways of reacting to external conditions.

Individual character is, therefore, not solely determined by the culture but rather by the impact of life's experiences on the unique temperament and physical constitution of an individual person. The psychological side is stressed by Fromm as he emphasizes the fact that if human behavior is not solely a matter of social conditioning we will have to do more than change social patterns to affect a change in human behavior.

The point Fromm seeks to make here should not be minimized. It is, of course, true that for a personality governed completely from without the habits and thought of such a personality will be the result of conforming to cultural patterns. When the character of the person is a heteronomously guided one (in this case by culture and society), it will probably be true that the weakness of the autonomous thrust will make such a person an easier candidate for manipulation by new social patterns. But for the self governed by a strong autonomous center and where its character is formed more from within than without, mere social planning is not a sufficient method to deal with the transcendent dimension of the self, which can stand above or outside a mere social manipulation or programming.

Totalitarian social schemes which seek to "remake" human nature in terms of a social principle need to be made aware of Fromm's point. The flaw in such schemes is not that the social ideal envisioned may not be a just one but that they fail to understand that human nature is something more than just clay to be molded as the social theorist may wish. A completely heteronomous personality, it is true, is nearer the "clay" principle, but persons are more than just clay. Kant's first universal law that persons should be treated as ends and not as means only reflects the ethical or moral side of this question. But Fromm appears to go deeper into the psycho-social dimensions than Kant. While Kant says we ought to treat persons as ends, Fromm says that the recognition of authentic selfhood means we cannot bypass the autonomous and self-transcendent dimensions of the person which are most forcibly seen in the freedom (through conscience and other ways) to resist social dictation. For example, totalitarian efforts at thought control are really a heteronomous structuring and sooner or later are bound to conflict with the autonomous freedom which seeks to break such chains.

It should be made clear that Fromm is not denying the social principle (after all, his major thesis is that we are primarily social beings). What he is saying is that a view that seeks to remake human nature solely through social or cultural conditioning is too simplistic an understanding of the interlocking relationship between persons and their social orders. He is, in fact, trying to tell us that a depth of understanding of human nature demands that something beyond a mere social technique is necessary.

The laws of our nature, as human persons, refer then in Fromm's view not only to biological equipment alone or to social patterns or culture alone but to our unique endowment and powers of self-transcendence. This is not to say that we are simply disembodied intellects. Rather, a human person is a multidimensional being and to reduce the person to any one dimension alone is a serious error.

As noted earlier, basic to Fromm's theory of value is his theory of productive orientation. We referred to this earlier in his theory of the self where he held that the isolated individual's reunification with the world has to be understood in terms of love and work.

We need to look first at the opposite of the productive, namely, the nonproductive types of orientation.

There are three types of nonproductive character orientations which Fromm alludes to: specifically, the receptive, exploitative, and hoarding orientations.

The receptive orientation is that of a person who looks outside himself and finds that to get what he wants he must look outside himself. In this orientation, Fromm says, "the problem of love is almost exclusively that of 'being loved' and not that of loving."[18] This is an example of a heavy dependency principle at work in which the self seeks its security outside itself, something which indicates lack of self-strength.

The exploitative orientation is that of grabbing and stealing. This type of view seems to see value in that which is attached to something else and seeks to take it away. If the object sought is not attached it loses its drawing power for the exploiter.

The hoarding orientation is that of a security based on hoarding and saving; spending is felt to be a threat. In this view, says Fromm, "love is essentially a possession; they do not give love but try to get it by possessing the beloved. . . ."[19] People are to be possessed, owned and have little being in their own right except as a satisfaction to the possessor. Persons are treated as means only, not as ends.

Fromm refers to the productive orientation of personality as involving a fundamental attitude, "a mode of relatedness," as he calls it, in all realms of experience. "Productiveness," says Fromm, "means that he experiences himself as the embodiment of his powers and as the 'actor'; that he feels himself one with his powers and at the same time that they are not masked and alienated from him."[20] Again, the productive character is that which is an originator of action not simply a reaction to something else as is the case with the pseudoself referred to earlier.

The productive orientation has to do with what Fromm terms *potency*. Potency is the power of reason to penetrate beneath phenomena to understand the essence of something; it is the power of love breaking through the walls that separate people; it is the power to visualize, through imagination, things not yet existing.

The failure to recognize and to develop this inner potency causes us to resort to something like a dominating mentality seeking to control others and things. In other words, the "controlling" type of mentality gives evidence that an inner potency principle has not been developed. Potency would indicate an originating strength in the self while the lack of it would imply a kind of weakness and insecurity. Thus, says Fromm, "domination springs from impotence and in turn reinforces it, for if an individual can force somebody to serve him, his own need to be productive is increasingly paralyzed."[21]

Perhaps the most important aspect of Fromm's theory of value is his view of productive love. This idea of love is much different from that which is frequently called love. He notes the ambiguous character of the word:

> There is hardly any word which is more ambiguous and confusing than the word "love." It is used to denote almost every feeling short of hate and disgust. It comprises everything from the love of ice cream to the love for a symphony, from mild sympathy to the most intense feeling of closeness. People feel they love if they have "fallen for" somebody. They call their dependence love, and their possessiveness, too.[22]

Genuine love, in Fromm's view, is rooted in productiveness. While he agrees that objects of love and intensity of love may differ, he nevertheless holds that certain basic elements may be said to be characteristic of all forms of productive love. These are, he says, "care, responsibility, respect, and knowledge."[23]

Fromm interprets love as a force which unites a human person with his or her world as well as with him or her self. "Love," Fromm suggests, "is union with somebody, or something, outside oneself, under the condition of retaining the separateness and integrity of one's own self. It is an experience of sharing, of communion, which permits the unfolding of one's own inner activity."[24]

Another aspect of his productive love idea is Fromm's analysis of conscience: specifically, what he calls two types of conscience and which he names the "authoritarian" conscience and the "humanistic" conscience. He defines the authoritarian conscience as basically the voice of an external authority which has internalized itself. Examples of such external authority could be parents, state, culture. The prescriptions of the authoritarian conscience are not determined by one's own value judgment but "exclusively by the fact that its commands and taboos are pronounced by authorities."[25] On the other hand, the humanistic conscience is not the internalized voice of an external authority whom we are eager to please or afraid to displease. It is, says Fromm, "our own voice, present in every human being and independent of external sanctions and rewards."[26]

In a conscience conditioned in the authoritarian way, the person feels guilty when he exercises his own strength, independence, productiveness, pride, and so forth. On the other hand, the "good" conscience in the authoritarian type is that which expresses the feeling of obedience, dependence, powerlessness, sinfulness, and so forth. The authoritarian tradition, then, develops those qualities which are not a reinforcement to the self-esteem or to the building of a healthy self-love.

Humanistic ethics bases its theory on the fact that if human persons are to have confidence in values, they must know themselves and the capacities of their own nature for productiveness and goodness. Man's unification with his world lies in the "productive orientation"—a mode of relatedness in which the human person is not masked and alienated from him or her self. Love, both for one's self and for others, is the best expression of the productive orientation since, according to Fromm, the integrity of the self is retained while a reunion with others is affirmed.

What implications does Fromm's theory of the self and theory of value carry for a theory of the social order? Or, what type of social order is most consistent with the majority of Fromm's theses? Let us turn now to a brief treatment of that area.

We need to note first that, in order for human fulfillment to occur in any sane way, the conditions must be present in society which encourage and promote self-fulfillment; that is, conditions that assist in the formation of self-esteem, healthy self-love, and respect for and integrity of the person. The opposite of this kind of social order is one in which the social conditions encourage domination and submission rather than brotherhood, conditions which serve to alienate us from other persons, conditions which reduce us to automatons, conditions where a person does not have an active say in the determination of the conditions under which one lives and works.

Fromm's Socialist humanism interprets Karl Marx as basically concerned with the self-alienation of man from himself. For him, genuine Marxism is a humanistic orientation rather than an authoritarian or totalitarian one. The Soviet type would be representative of a highly authoritarian political order, a bureaucratic structure in which the humanist stress on human rights and freedom of thought seem minimized. Likewise, he sees Chinese Marxism as highly totalitarian in character. These presentations of Marxism are in Fromm's view not genuinely humanistic in character and thus not in an original Marxist tradition. They are distortions.

To be sure, there are those who disagree with Fromm's interpretation of Marx as basically humanistic.[27] But the primary thrust of Fromm's argument grows out of a strong emphasis on the place and importance and value of the individual person. He says at one point, for example, that Marx was really a "spiritual existentialist" because he holds that the chief thrust of Marx's thought was the alienation of the individual in the modern industrial state and that our purpose must be to recapture for the individual person a social and economic order where a person is at one with his work and life. The person in that order would be the person as both actor and participant.

Such a social order would reflect the humanistic ideal: "a system of thought and feeling centered upon man, his growth, integrity, dignity, freedom; upon man as an end in himself, and not as a means toward anything; upon his capacity to be active not only as an individual but as a participant in history. . . ."[28]

Alienation is a state in which the individual is set over/against the world outside him; the loss of a sense of unity and communion with the objects of his labor produces a distancing in which the human person does not experience himself as an acting agent in his world. His being becomes dehumanized as he becomes a number, a cog in the wheel, a "means only" to things beyond his control and over which he has no say. Productive relatedness is lost and the consequent insecurity, aloneness and lostness moves us in the direction of giving up the striving for individual fulfillment and freedom. Persons feel an increasing worthlessness and loss of their own integrity.

The integrity and worth, then, must be rebuilt on positive relations. Love becomes a principle of connection—the relating in terms of active participation builds the self and its worth. The less there is of productive connection the more alienated and lost the self becomes. This is Fromm's primary thesis: that we are primarily social beings and the authenticity of our selfhood rests on positive productive relationships in which we feel a unity with our work and world.

Having surveyed Fromm's philosophy of the self and value, I return to the introductory comment. There we confronted a core problem, namely: How are individual needs, hopes, dreams, and thoughts to be squared with other individuals whose same needs do not coincide with one's own? The answer to the question assumes, of course, that our existential condition suggests some sort of pluralism in human life and organization rather than the stultifying uniformity which would be characteristic of a group of robots socially programmed and controlled. In the structuring of a social order, how do we keep that structure from becoming an impositionistic form which blocks my freedom to be what *I* think I need to be?

I think Fromm is on the right track with his emphasis on love both of self and others as the guide. But more analysis needs to be done on how one resolves the knotty problem of my own needs, wants, and thoughts (i.e., my freedom to be *me*) when they are on collision course with social structures and social systems. For example, what place shall give to "right of conscience" in the face of the social pressures for conformity?

Granted, one could say that the social system should be such that it will not collide with, but rather fulfill, my autonomous meanings and values. But how do you have a social system which satisfies the multitude of existential or individual orientations about what one should do, be, or have? Love may be the kind of principle we are seeking if by love we mean a basic respect for the autonomy of all others so that each person "doing *his* or *her* thing" will be careful not to interfere with the others "doing *their* thing."

It is clear, then, that the freedom issue poses real problems. It is one thing to say that the life of the human person must be a freedom to fulfill him or her self and have a social order which protects and encourages that right. But are you not immediately thrust into a moral and value-theory problem of individual meaning and value as over and against universal principles and structures which seem necessary for social order? How much order is necessary to protect the freedom? The emergence of societies and cultures occurs at least partly because a more universal principle governing individual relationships is essential as protection against "unbridled" individualism.

Surely, social structures may often block human fulfillment, so our essential task would seem to be: work for a society that provides the economic, political, and social conditions that best meet the demand for *both* human fulfillment and freedom.

A radical existentialism provides the philosophical base for a stress on individual life and meaning but it does not provide, in my estimation, enough of a connectional principle to help us resolve the problem of human beings relating to each other. Fromm's commendable effort is in the direction toward the cutting of a pattern for a resolution of the part-whole problem of our existence and he struggles, therefore, with how love could be the key to both individual and social fulfillment.

Bibliography

Fromm, Erich. *Escape from Freedom* (New York: Holt, Rinehart & Winston, 1941).

Fromm, Erich. *Man for Himself: An Inquiry into the Psychology of Ethics* (New York: Holt, Rinehart & Winston, 1947).

Fromm, Erich. *Psychoanalysis and Religion* (New Haven: Yale University Press, 1950).

Fromm, Erich. *The Forgotten Language: An Introduction to the Understanding of Dreams, Fairytales, and Myths* (New York: Holt, Rinehart & Winston, 1951).

Fromm, Erich. *The Sane Society* (New York: Holt, Rinehart & Winston, 1955).

Fromm, Erich. *Sigmund Freud's Mission* (New York: Harper, 1959).

Fromm, Erich. *Marx's Concept of Man* (New York: Ungar, 1961).

Fromm, Erich. *The Heart of Man* (New York: Harper & Row, 1964).

Fromm, Erich. *The Revolution of Hope* (New York: Harper & Row, 1968).

Fromm, Erich. *The Crisis of Psychoanalysis: Essays on Freud, Marx, and Social Psychology* (New York: Holt, Rinehart & Winston, 1970).

Fromm, Erich. *The Anatomy of Human Destructiveness* (New York: Holt, Rinehart & Winston, 1973).

Chapter 6

Socialism
and the Arts

Marxism and Kazantzakis*
by N. Georgopoulos

Nikos Kazantzakis, the renowned Greek writer, criticized communism for its worship of the machine and its emphasis on analytical reason and practical goals. From a Spenglerian-Bergsonian perspective, he also criticized both dialectical materialism and scientific socialism. At the same time, he considered Marx as the lawgiver of our age and communism as the reality defining our times, a reality whose significance he found in its constituting a stage of transition between the bourgeois culture and a culture yet to come. Communism is seen both as the single, latest, and most powerful force in the dissolution of the bougeois civilization which already had its high point and is at the final stage of its downard curve of decline, as well, and at the same time, as itself being that final stage. As such, communism has created, or rather is, an interregnum, on the other side of which Kazantzakis could see the vague adumbrations of a new era. One which, although it is to transcend the Communist reality we are presently living, cannot be thought of as coming to be realized without having first gone through that reality. This new era Kazantzakis called metacommunism.

I fight to embrace the entire circle of human activity to the full extent of my ability, to divine which wind is urging all these waves of mankind upward. I bend over the age in which I live, that tiny, imperceptible arc of the vast circle, and struggle to attain a clear view of today's duty. Perhaps this is the only way man can carry out something immortal within the ephemeral moment of his life: immortal because he collaborates with an immortal rhythm. *(Report to Greco)*

---

*This article appeared in *Byzantine and Modern Greek Studies,* vol. 3 (1977), pp. 175-200. Reprinted by permission of the editors.

The name of Nikos Kazantzakis continues to arouse controversy. Much of it, especially in Greece, is political in nature and revolves around the confusion concerning Kazantzakis' relation to Marxism. The confusion arises because of the ways Kazantzakis' activities and writings have been interpreted. For example, even before the latest military regime in Greece and while he was still alive, Kazantzakis was an anathema to the royalists. Consecutive right-wing governments, both before and after World War II, waged war against him and his books; he was called immoral, red, and a Bolshevik troublemaker.[1] In the fall of 1924, in his native Crete, he was actually arrested. In the spring of 1928, in Athens, he was accused of being a Russian agent.[2] Yet his books were banned in Russia—particularly those he wrote about that country—and the Greek Communist party refused to include him in its ranks, labeling him bourgeois, decadent, and even Fascist. In fact, his offer to join the Communist-controlled resistance in the 1940s was rejected. Such responses neither prevented the International Peace Committee from offering him the Peace Award in Vienna in 1956 nor did it bar the Chinese Communists from inviting him to the People's Republic of China as one of their "chosen foreigners," and, upon the occasion of his death in 1957, from praising him: "Kazantzakis was not only a great writer. He was actively interested in social and political issues. He was also a devotee of peace."[3] More recently views about him have ranged from those in which he is considered an egomaniac, oblivious to the fate of others, a man for whom "the really important things—political tyranny, social injustice, economic exploitation—interested him the least,"[4] to those in which he is seen as an advocate of equality, peace, and the cooperation of the world's people, one who to the end of his career sided with the "ideas of genuine democracy and socialism."[5]

By examining Kazantzakis' views in connection with Marxism and by delineating his attitude and approach to the subject—"a very complicated affair,"[6] as he himself put it—an attempt will be made to clear up the confusing and even antithetical interpretations about his views, and thus to eliminate some of the prejudices that continue to plague the name of the greatest man of letters of modern Greece.

I will do this first by providing evidence of Kazantzakis' affinities with Marxism. Second, I will outline his basic disagreements, criticism, and objections to Marxism, objections which seem to be in conflict with his expressed espousals; out of these seemingly contradictory positions, I will present what appears to me to be the truth concerning his relation to Marxism. Finally, I will argue that this true relation did not alter during his lifetime; I will emphasize that it was not merely one stage, among others, punctuating his development, but constituted a facet of his variegated but organically unified thought.

Kazantzakis' affinities with Marxism began when he was a student in Paris There, he had become acquainted with and was impressed by young French Socialists. However, as his newspaper dispatches of those years show, his main attraction to socialism was limited to its being a substitute for the decaying values of Christianity: "The Socialists address themselves to the needs of contemporary man because they base their program on the death of Christian otherworldliness. They attempt to improve this life since none other exists."[7] His early flirtation with French socialism did not last long because he was not only influenced by Nietzsche, but also consumed by zeal for his own country. In the 1910s, under the influence of I. Dragoumis and E. Venizelos, and caught by the fervor of Greece's recovery of its lands from the Turks, he became involved in rehabilitating Greece primarily through educational reforms. In 1919, as director general of the Ministry of Welfare, he successfully undertook the repatriation of 150,000 Greeks from the Caucasus.

However, he would not remain long in Greece. The year 1920 was arduous both for him and his country. Dragoumis was assassinated; Venizelos fell from power. Dissatisfied with the Greek political situation, Kazantzakis traveled to Vienna; his attention turned toward the Soviet Union. The attraction of the "Russian experiment" was powerful, and the Vienna of 1921 provided scenes that propelled Kazantzakis to search for a robust unapologetic communism. Witness the correspondence with his first wife; referring to the experiences of misery and indignity he witnesses in post World War I Vienna he writes:

Now with our new perception [the acceptance of communist ideas] you don't know with what emotion I see the people here suffering from hunger and despair. What unhappiness, my God, and how long would it last? Today, for example, I went to buy a newspaper, and a little girl of about fourteen entered with a sack full of packages which she was carrying on her back. I went to help her unload it and couldn't lift it. The little girl smiled, but her body was already deformed, her shoulders hunched, her legs were like reeds. . . .

I look at the paintings, the beautiful bibelots, that are in the shop windows. At another time, as early even as last year they used to give me joy. Now, I feel how unnatural they are, superficial masks to hide the truth. Seductive personae for the cowards. My God! I shout inside me while walking the broad avenues, when are you going to descend like a tempestuous wind, like the Great One who descends from the mountain tops of Parnassus, to clear up the earth?[8]

Six months later his letters continue in the same vein. Describing the social conditions in Vienna, he writes: "Here we have children who gather around the entrances of big hotels and as soon as the door is left open they run under the tables and pick up the crumbs. And next to them we have the shamelessness of the rich, gypsy music, dances, cabarets, and the people red-faced and fat from steaks."[9]

In the same month he puts the contrast in political terms and for the first time informs us of his initiation into Communist circles:

I have found a man to get me in touch with the local Communists. . . . I hope to see the overthrow here soon. It is impossible to imagine the intensity which the horror has reached. . . .[10]

As these tumultuous years pass by, as the shame and suffering he witnesses in Vienna become his own, as his "thirst for justice" increases, we hear him become more and more immersed in Communist ideas and see him possessed by the revolutionary fervor enveloping the Germany of the times. Moving from Vienna to Berlin, he joins a group of rebels and soon renews his plans already begun in Vienna for the publication of a leftist periodical, *Nova Graecia,* "in order to initiate from here the coming awakening—the human one."[11] He reads Communist books, participates in street demonstrations, and expresses his opinions at meetings of Communists and extreme Socialists. Of these meetings he writes to his wife, "the others insist principally on the cultivation of selected intellectuals who will be able to handle philosophical, scientific, cultural, etc., themes from a Communist, Marxist perspective. I insist on the necessity to leave alone for now all these intellectual luxuries and see how we would address ourselves (1) to the people in general, (2) to the workers in particular, (3) to the children."[12]

Even after he leaves Berlin in 1924, and travels through Germany and northern Italy to Assisi, his letters continue to express his mounting enthusiasm for what he had initially called his "new perception": communism. He hopes to fight against "decadence and misery." He writes disparagingly of the "dishonorable capitalistic system" that governs France.[13] Later from Assisi, he goes as far as to refer to Saint Francis as "a great, an ideal Communist. He saw that the source of all evil is private property."[14] He speaks of his new development, his awakening to internationalism, in terms that he will staunchly advocate throughout his life:

> In the beginning men care only for their ego, then for their family and their home, and then for the race and the fatherland. Lastly they care for Man himself. There always existed men, in all epochs, from Prometheus to Lenin, who fought for Man. But their struggle was isolated, scattered, luciferian; they did not induce the universal masses. Now we must struggle to consolidate this new army, to teach (by first giving the example) the world's people to breathe outside of their borders and to feel pain and joy when the men in Russia and China feel pain and joy.[15]

Later, reflecting a developing consciousness of history, he refers to our times as those of a new Middle Age which must be gone through before the appearance of a new, free, higher civilization.[16]

In 1924, this correspondence ceased; Kazantzakis left southern Italy for Crete. It was in Crete that his sentiments for Socialist causes were publicly expressed. The consequence was a strong reaction on the part of the authorities. At Herakleion, carried off by his enthusiasm and his Messianic spirit, he became involved with the local Communists in what the authorities viewed as an illegal political action, and was arrested. However, what is of interest to us here is neither the action in which he took part, nor the fact of his being accused, but the "Confession of Faith" which he submitted to the examining magistrate of Herakleion when he was arrested as a Communist. This "confession" was to become his "Apology."

In this document the thoughts which Kazantzakis had expressed at times desultorily in his letters, mingled as they were with so many other issues and private concerns, became summarized and crystallized into a clear statement. In it he states unambiguously that the established bourgeois system is no longer capable of adjusting itself to contemporary needs and the concerns of society. Economically, this system is based on predatory private relations of production and on the unequal distribution of wealth; socially, there does not exist a single ethos to support the relations between men; politically, the ruling class administers political power to its own benefit and at the expense of the majority. Moreover, he continues, there does not exist in the bourgeois system a lofty ideal, a faith, a suprapersonal rhythm which can give dignity and cohesion to the activities and energies of individuals and nations. Granting that the bourgeois class, having overturned feudalism, contributed admirably to thought, art, science, and action, he observes that now it is embarked on its fateful, downward curve. Although we may not clearly perceive this curve (since we are living in it), two different kinds of endeavors are becoming obvious. On the one hand, there are those who are struggling to overturn and replace this situation with "a new system, which, they are convinced, is more just and more honorable."[17] On the other hand, the former, according to Kazantzakis, are fighting a well-expected, but losing, battle. They disregarded the implacable and vital historical laws of birth, growth, and decline. They hope that now, for the first time in history, their class can be maintained forever in power—a vain miracle. Yet what kind of class would succeed the bourgeoisie? He answers:

> I have the adamantine conviction that it will be the working class: workers, farmers, people productive in the spirit. This class has passed the first stage—charity. It no longer, as a century ago, kowtows to the charity of the rich people, no longer begs for alms. And then it passed the second stage—Justice; no longer is it demanding to seize the ruling power because that is right. And now it has reached the third and final stage; it is convinced that it will assume the ruling power, because such is the historical necessity.[18]

He now considered it his duty to make his contemporaries aware of the "new rhythm of on-going life. How? By articulating a clear idea of the historical moment we are passing through, by enlightening the people and by giving a new and loftier content to the conceptions of work, justice, virtue."[19]

Kazantzakis thought he could bring about an awareness in himself by first forming a clear and impartial idea of "the greatest contemporary problem which regulates our era—the Russian problem."[20] But he had to see with his own eyes, get his own impressions, form his own thoughts. For he felt that unlike other times of calmness when one had the right to withdraw into solitude, "at the critical moment we are living, I knew it was man's duty to take, in full consciousness and with decisiveness, a stand—to the left or right—in the universal battle." It would have been an "abominable cowardice," he concludes in the "Apology," to do otherwise. In October of 1925 he left for Russia.

The tone of his letters, the explicit statements of his "Apology," his three trips to Russia and his activities there and in Greece reveal his growing loyalties and forcefully challenge the accusation that the Greek writer was oblivious to the fate of others and uninterested in political tyranny, social injustice and economic exploitation. As we have seen, it was precisely such interests, triggered as they were by the social, political, and economic conditions in Germany and Vienna in the early 1920s, that engendered his Marxist sentiments and forged his initial commitments to Lenin and the Russian revolution.

On his second visit to Russia, as an officially invited guest to the tenth anniversary of the revolution, he participated in the pro-Communist World Congress by expressing his convictions about one of the main issues discussed: the threat of a new world war. He disagreed with the prevalent view among the delegates that such a war should be avoided by organizing the world proletariat to refuse to fight against each other. He argued, to the contrary, that there was only one thing that the world proletariat could and must do: prepare for it and, when it comes, turn the capitalist war into a social one.[21]

Later, in Greece, with Panait Istrati[22] (a writer and a new-found friend), and D. Glynos (the leading intellectual of the Left at the time), Kazantzakis organized a large meeting at the Alhambra theater where both he and Istrati spoke. Their speeches touched a revolutionary nerve in the audience which, applauding and shouting, marched to the center of Athens singing the "Third International." Three days after the Alhambra incident the public prosecutor ordered an investigation of the three agitators, accusing Istrati of being a Communist agent. Istrati was asked to leave the country and a trial date was set for Glynos and Kazantzakis, but it was repeatedly postponed and finally forgotten.[23]

In the spring of 1928 Kazantzakis met again with Istrati in Kiev. Together they planned to journey through the entire country and write articles for the world press. The articles were to be about the struggle of "crucified Russia" and plans were made to have them published in three volumes entitled "Following the Red Star." To this end, in Borjom and later in Tiflis, Kazantzakis wrote some forty articles. "I am going to send most of them," he wrote to Prevelakis, "to *Nouvelles Literaires,* but do not know whether they will publish them. As for them, they are revolutionary, here in Russia they are regarded as *mystiques.*"[24]

However, these articles were never published. By the time Kazantzakis and Istrati reached Leningrad, Istrati underwent a test of faith which had been brewing for some time; the two friends became estranged.[25] The crisis developed when the Soviet government officially accused Istrati's old friend, the Russian writer Victor Serge, of Trotskyism. Istrati was outraged. He violently protested to the government, met with officials, and spoke to party members—to no avail. Serge was exiled; his wife went mad and his family was literally abandoned to the streets. Istrati was heartbroken. His hopes about Russia shattered, he angrily withdrew the vow, given no more than a year before, to serve Russia to the end of his life.[26] Returning to Paris, he destroyed all the articles written by Kazantzakis and co-signed by him which were intended for publication in European periodicals.

Kazantzakis was no doubt disturbed by Serge's fate and the whole "Rusakov Affair," as it came to be called. Yet the point from which Kazantzakis was viewing Bolshevik Russia was all too encompassing to let this incident and others like it affect his overall position vis-à-vis the "Russian experiment." Unlike Istrati, who

all too soon became disillusioned by the Russian reality, Kazantzakis did not consider this a fixed state of affairs. It was still
fluid, still "in a state of becoming. The Russian reality is replete
with contradictions, facts that are logically inexplicable and remnants of all realities. . . . Things are just beginning to live and
still have all the awkwardness, the complexity and the charm of a
newborn baby."[27] And in a section in *Toda Raba,* which no doubt
refers to the time just before Istrati's departure, Kazantzakis,
reflecting on his friend's all too human reaction, has Geranos say:
"Beyond logic, beyond discussions and disputes, beyond economic
needs and party programs, higher than the Soviets and the Com-
missars, the force at work in the USSR and controlling it is the
dark, intemperate ruthless Spirit of our age."[28]

Such words make clear that Kazantzakis was interested not
in Soviet communism as such, not in a dogmatic intellectual Marxism, but in the revolutionary spirit he saw at work in Russia. "It
is not Russia that interests me," Geranos says in *Toda Raba,* "but
the flame consuming Russia."[29] In a letter from Moscow in 1925,
a month before he concluded his first trip to the Soviet Union, he
expressed the same sentiment when he wrote that what moved
him in Russia was not "the reality they had achieved but the
reality which they long for and do not know that they cannot
achieve."[30]

Kazantzakis' attitude toward Russia and communism—an attitude which grew out of his horror in the face of the injustices he
found in the capitalist system—illuminates his affinity for communism and seems to warrant the identification of him as "red"
and "Bolshevik."

In spite of Kazantzakis' seeming allegiances to the "Russian
experiment" and the great importance he attached to communism,
the Communists also had something on their side when they
rejected him as bourgeois and decadent and when the Russian
government prohibited the circulation of his books, for he was
never a Communist. It is this simple fact that presents us with
difficulties in assessing his relation to Marxism and continues to
confuse matters regarding his position.

The explicit statement in *Toda Raba,* that he was not a party
member blinded by a complacent faith, is not the only evidence

of his not being a Communist.[31] In a letter to Prevelakis in 1936 explaining his "spiritual longitude and latitude," he wrote that although he belonged to the left wing he was "never a Communist."[32] And in a conversation with Istrati which he recorded in his *Russia,* he denied the latter's claim that he, Kazantzakis, was a Marxist.[33]

It is simplistic and debatable to say with Prevelakis that the reason Kazantzakis was not a communist was because "the narrow-minded and strong Communist dedicated to action . . . [the] person who desposed of metaphysics and was ignorant of the inner life and who mocked at the adventure of love . . ." that this kind of man, "the new type of man produced in Russia appalled him."[34] Ample evidence in his writing suggests that far from being appalled by the man of action, Kazantzakis had a great and lasting admiration for him. Although he himself was nurtured by Western art and philosophy, and may have even, as Prevelakis put it, "personified broad polyhedral thought," he often spoke with sarcasm and derision about the "metaphysical problem"[35] and about the atrophied Western intellectuals (like the boss in *Zorba the Greek*) whose neutrality, objectivity, and noninvolvement were fostering the decadence of Western civilization. Witness the important essay sent to Prevelakis in the form of a letter in which he stresses that as a result of his trips to Russia he had ultimately discovered that his nature was not that of a man of action; he nevertheless "knows how full the life of a man can also be today who dedicates himself to action uprooting superfluous and minute aesthetic and metaphysical objections."[36]

We must also guard against the impression given by Prevelakis' brief comments that Kazantzakis was hostile to Marxism because of its conception of the new man; Kazantzakis, in Prevelakis' eyes, personified and represented Western tradition while the new type of man, the Marxist, was ignorant of and despised the humanist values of that tradition. For Kazantzakis, the so-called new man, the committed Communist, was not new at all. In the final analysis and from the large perspective, Marxism had little or nothing new to offer. Far from being a change in the fighting front of the human battle (as he himself might have thought before his trip to Russia and as the Communists themselves might have wanted to believe), communism was another extension of Western culture, in fact "the most extreme and most logical consequence of bourgeois civilization."[37]

According to Marx, communism was to be the necessary consequence of the capitalist civilization, the final stage of the material dialectic of history. However, this is not what Kazantzakis had in mind; it is not what he meant when considering communism the logical consequence of bourgeois civilization. What he did mean was that communism, as a faith based on the theoretical interpretations and conceptions of Marx, did not lead to the novelty that the dialectical method implies, but merely logically carried some aspects of the bourgeois culture to their final consequences. More specifically, he explicitly pointed to the two basic aspects which comprise its main characteristics: the materialistic conception of life, and the worship of the machine. In fact, if the United States is seen from this perspective (the final achievement of Western bourgeois culture), then "the ideal of Soviet Russia is America,"[38] with only one difference: the fairer distribution of material goods. "The bourgeois civilization, with its development of critical intelligence, demolished all religions and created that which we call science, i.e., rules by which we can know and can subjugate the natural powers. Communism defies all these fruits of bourgeois endeavor and attempts only to carry out—and does carry out—a more just distribution of material goods."[39]

For Kazantzakis, the mission of communism, far from being the creation of a new culture, was only the swan song of the old one, the final stage of the decomposition of bourgeois civilization. "Communism is the end, not the beginning. It has all the symptoms of the end: extreme materialism, hypertrophy of the rational, deadly analysis of every belief which transcends the five senses, deification of practical goals."[40]

His criticism of the materialism of communism was not limited to the worship of the machine and the emphasis on the practical, but went to its theoretical roots in Marxism. Kazantzakis disagreed vigorously with the most fundamental thesis of Marx's dialectical materialism—the notion that societies are and have been governed by the prevailing means of production; or more generally, that economics constitutes the absolute foundation of the socio-political and spiritual superstructure and is the reason and cause of any change. He agreed that the economic factors play a central role in the unfolding of a people's history and that economics is one of the most powerful movers of human life, if for no other reason than that it serves man's basic needs—"man has always the need to eat." But more often than not there are factors other than economics that dominate and determine the historical unfolding and destiny of a people: "religion, race, historical adventures, the appearance of a great figure." For example, he did not believe that we can explain the appearance and unexpected triumph of the Mohammedan civilization by appealing exclusively to the economic conditions of the Arab world in the seventh century. "The same economic conditions had weighed down the people of the Arab race for many centuries . . . and suddenly one man, a great figure is born . . . the unforeseen is ready every moment to open a different path in history. . . . What sudden invincible force was impelling these people? Certainly not only economic motives but a deeper force, richer and irascible—a faith."[41] Similarly he did not agree that we can explain the causes responsible for the Christian civilization as economic in character.

According to Kazantzakis, an historian can prove what he wishes, given the weight of his central premise and principles of selection. But if we objectively and impartially look at the history of humanity, we will see that all these causes together "mold humanity and now one dominates, now the other, now many or all together in hard-to-analyze percentages of contribution."[42]

Not only did Kazantzakis disagree with Marxism by not considering the economic factors the sole and basic causes in determining the structure and direction of a culture, he also saw them as sometimes being effects—results or outcomes of a number of factors. It is the working together of these factors (such as "race, luck, climate, wars, an invention, and many others") that creates a given set of economic motives and conditions. These conditions are often merely the visible forms of deeper urges and invisible forces—forces which because of their fluidity and opacity cannot be used as easy slogans for the masses.

Finally, he considered it, if not totally arbitrary, certainly narrow to hold with Marxists that art, morality, and thought are the effects of economic laws and material conditions and that changes in the latter necessarily bring about changes in the former. Could it perhaps be the case, he asks rhetorically, "that the moral and spiritual changes are results which preexist, much earlier than the economic change."[43] It was only, he thought, because the economic changes come to be discerned first that Marxism superficially takes them to be the primary causes and all other changes as their effects.

Above all, it was what he took to be the dogmatism of historical dialectical materialism that offended his sensibility and ran contrary to his own conception of things—its one-sidedness as to what determines historical eras and directs humanity on the one hand, and on the other its "prophecy" as to the definite and permanent solution of man's problems. Not only, according to Marxism, are the means of production (i.e., the economic factors) the sole causes determining the social and ideological superstructure, the appropriate regulation of which would lead to socialism, but as is well known, the latter will invariably have to pass through two stages of evolutionary unfolding: the stage which Marx calls in his *Economic and Philosophical Manuscripts* "crude communism" and the stage of "pure communism."

Kazantzakis objected to both what he understood to be the idea of the termination of the social evolution in "pure communism" and to the promises it was thought to contain. He derogatorily referred to this dogmatic antidialectic contained in the promises of "pure communism" as "The Iron Law"[44] and considered it to be one of the weakest points of Marxism. For him, as we are going to see shortly, the historical dialectic or "the undulating pattern of history" has no end, passing through a ceaseless series of "decays, births, high points, declines, decays," to an endless renewal of life and civilizations. Although ultimately quite different in his convictions from Engels, he would have agreed with the latter's statement that "all successive historical situations are only transitory stages in an endless course of development from the lower to the higher."[45]

Kazantzakis' rejection of the fundamental notions of historical materialism necessarily followed from his rejection of what he considered to be the naive scientific determination that underlies it. Influenced as he was by Bergson's philosophy, he could not accept the claim of orthodox scientific socialism that social (i.e., human) phenomena can be determined and predicted in a way analogous to those of the empirical sciences. The methods of the physical sciences could in no sense be applied to life. If life or life's reality is, as he believed it to be, a ceaselessly changing process, always moving ahead and forever creating newness and novelty, then life's phenomena, unlike the merely physical ones, cannot be taken up and arranged without being drastically distorted; nor can they be framed mathematically. Life is a ceaseless dynamic process; we cannot establish its laws. Laws, he observed, are made from repetitions, while life—and this is its qualitative difference from matter—is continual creation: the birth of something new which was not included in what was previously given. "But never, under no circumstances, can in life the very same causes repeat themselves and therefore the same effects be predicted. And since the phenomena of life cannot be brought under laws then science, that is to say, systems of laws, cannot possibly exist in the case of social phenomena."[46] Far from being able to determine and predict the future of social events, a science of society, e.g., scientific socialism, can only interpret past events as past, as finished and dead, after they have already ceased to flow and unfold creatively. Such a science can only purport to anatomize life's cadaver; as such its value is only and significantly retrospective. It can analyze finished events and establish laws; but precisely because we cannot identify the inert "body of an era with the enormous breath that gives it life."[47] Its researches and interpretations cannot become lessons for the future. Therefore, such a science cannot be considered as a valuable guide for our thought and action.

We need not consider further his criticism of the theoretical foundations of Marxism, nor, for that matter, need we evaluate it to see that it, along with his explicit denial of being a Communist, flies in the face of the previous evidence presented. Were

these two sides to Kazantzakis' attitude toward "the greatest
contemporary problem regulating our era?" Was the confusion
of his interpreters a reflection of a fundamental ambiguity in Kazantzakis himself? Was he lying? Or did the two seemingly contradictory stands reflected two different periods of his development; that
the initial enthusiasm of his letters and "Apology" dwindled in the
light of a more critical and mature attitude?

Kazantzakis' criticism of theoretical Marxism did not prevent him from recognizing the real significance of Marx and the
crucial place his doctrine occupied in the course of historical reality. He continued to consider Marx the greatest figure of our
times. In the essay he sent to Prevelakis he referred to Marx as
the "legislator of the era" and as the "Supreme Ruler of our
times."[48] Not, as we have seen, because he absolutely agreed
with the theoretical aspects of Marxism; but because he saw
Marx's doctrine as constituting contemporary reality, as being
the signal of the times. Every period which has created a civilization had, according to Kazantzakis, its own slogan. In order for
it to have been the appropriate one, it had both to answer and
exaggerate the needs of the times. Furthermore, the slogan had
to be formulated simply. "For our time," he wrote in the same
essay, "this slogan is, beyond any doubt, the Communist slogan.
It has all the above characteristics: it answers to and exaggerates
today's reality."[49] As we have seen Kazantzakis explain, life,
reality, in and by itself, is too dynamic to have the logical and
fixed structures Marx assigned to it. He did not believe that
there existed, for instance, two classes so absolutely fixed with
such distinct lines of demarcation between them, forming two
completely separate camps. Yet Marx served a historical purpose: with a high-handedness verging on arrogance he forced
that reality into molds which he himself had *a priori* carved with
rigorous and precise logic. By framing the two classes he helped
them abruptly separate, acquire class consciousness, and, with it,
begin to place themselves in camps which his logic had already
prescribed. In doing so "Marx found the proper slogan for our
times by means of which he organized the masses: he gave them
a faith."[50]

The indisputable significance of Marx, according to Kazantzakis, resides precisely in this: in his having provided a faith
for his times such that the reality of the times is defined by it.
Kazantzakis might not have been in full agreement with the philosophical grounds of the signal, but he recognized it as the overwhelming force determining the contemporary world rhythm:
"For the first time in history, the earth is acquiring a unified.
consciousness. All races—white, black, yellow—are organized
around the same purpose."[51] He may not have accepted the promises claimed by that faith, but he was convinced that it was preparing the grounds for the final stage of decay of the decomposing
bourgeois civilization. In doing so, it was creating a transitional
period toward something higher in the climb of the human spirit.
It was ushering in an upward movement in the intractable and
ever-renewed laws of life and civilization: birth, high point, decline.

The reason Kazantzakis was awed by Russia and the reason
he went there was that for him it was the place where the activities
of the transitional period were beginning to be enacted: "where
man is striving, seeking, testing, experimenting to find out—to
open a path between the old world his soul can no longer tol-
erate and the new ideal that is struggling in vain to arrive." For
Kazantzakis it was this striving, these efforts to break the molds
of a past that had hardened and become inhuman; it was these
moments at which what had turned to dead matter was being
transubstantiated by human effort into Spirit that constituted
man's highest, "holiest" moments, the moments of change and
upward climb as he called them. There had been such moments
before in man's history. "Today it is Russia that is opening a
path, amidst hunger and blood, in order to raise life higher." Gen-
eralizing the same theme, he sums it up this way:

> For years now an unswerving belief has been taking hold of me,
> lighting up my insides: Someone struggling is climbing uphill
> from matter to plants, from plants to animals, from animals to
> man and is fighting for freedom. In every critical historical
> period, this Struggling One takes on a new face. Today the face
> it has taken is this: Leader of the World Proletariat.[52]

We should not be misled however, when we try to determine the extent to which, according to Kazantzakis, Russia had
opened—or actually discerned the nature of—the path it was try-

ing to open. Although Kazantzakis had repeatedly stated that the "amazing Soviet experiment" was the one which was shaping the great contemporary international reality, that reality was not an end in itself but comprised a stage of transition. "We live," he wrote at the end of his book on Russia, "from the Russian Revolution onward, the harrowing and bloody labor pains of some higher civilization." He left it to be understood that that civilization was not yet born, was not being realized in Russia and was not embodied in the Communist ideology or the premises of Marxist theory: "We live and therefore do not perceive our times. But centuries hence they will surely not be called renaissance but middle ages. Middle ages, that is to say, interregnum: one civilization is breaking and falling, the other is being born. The one is dying, for generations gasping, the other is in labor, for generations laboring."[53] The civilization which is dying is none other than the Western bourgeois civilization, and communism, as Kazantzakis saw it, constitutes the final stage of its dying process. It is here, as we saw earlier, that Kazantzakis places the significance of communism in the "undulating pattern of history." It is the single, latest, and most powerful force in the dissolution of a culture which already had its high point and is at the final stage of its downward curve of decline and decay; and at the same time and almost paradoxically it itself is that final stage.

Viewed from the global perspective Kazantzakis was trying to develop, communism has created—or rather is—an interregnum on the other side of which he could see the vague adumbrations of a new era: an era which, although it is to transcend the Communist reality we are presently experiencing, cannot be thought of as coming to be realized without having first gone through that reality. Kazantzakis chose, with deliberate ambiguity, to call this new age metacommunism. He must have had this in mind when he had stated earlier that the Communist experiment was opening a new path in order to raise life to a higher order.

Now, perhaps, we are in a better position to understand Kazantzakis' exhortation in the letter to Prevelakis, in the introduction to the French edition of *Toda Raba,* and elsewhere, that in the time in which we are living, one ought to be Communist. However, he qualifies this view: we must be Communists, but enlightened ones, implacable, without any shallow hope or simple-minded, superficial optimism. "We should not be like the naive Communists who think that happiness and justice will follow upon the triumph of communism."[54] Therefore, we could say that we ought to be Communists first because communism is, as we have seen, what defines contemporary reality; second, because by being Communists we will destroy the already crumbling bourgeois civilization and help mankind to move further into the transitional period; and third, because the further we move into that period and draw out the consequences of communism, the sooner we shall go through it and transcend it. "It is like the driver," Kazantzakis explained using the same example in more than one place, "who enters a burning forest. Instead of going back he should double his speed in order to get out of the fire. In the same way, we have entered this fearsome period and we must, as much as we can, stretch the implications of communism to their extreme consequences so that salvation may come sooner. What salvation? The destruction of this world and the beginning of the creation of another, with different foundations, where the worship of the machine, of logic and of practical goals will be considered worthless goods [sic]. A new slogan."[55]

At a time when the world was still in shock from the Bolshevik revolution and when Russia was at its first stage of applying Marxist theory, Kazantzakis was already drawing the consequences of communism and calling for a new signal and a new beginning. He considered it his right and duty as a man of thought to divine the new post-Marxist signal and to detect and salvage the potentialities in communism in order to use them as signposts for the future development of man. "If, however, we are not men of action, then we have the right, if we can, to wish for, to experience from now on and to divine this metacommunist slogan. Communism is the end but naturally like every end has in it many elements of the future beginning. What are these elements? From all our wishes and needs and presentiments that surround us which ones will survive and be used in the coming civilization? From all these emphemeral visions, which ones have the likelihood of relative immortality? This is the great agony and the great duty of today's creative theorist."[56]

Commentators often speak of the influences certain great figures exerted on Kazantzakis' intellectual development and quite as often see that development in terms of clearly defined stages. Kazantzakis himself was partially responsible for this since in more than one place he had explicitly acknowledged his debt to the great men who aided him in his long and "bloody journey": Christ, Buddha, Nietzsche, Bergson, Lenin, Odysseus. Such admissions on his part, however, given the nature of his thought, are more prone to mislead than to enlighten: they tend to be interpreted in such a way as to suggest that his thought is a mere conglomeration of the philosophical attitudes reflected by these great names. In their attempt to determine the nature, force, and time of these influences, commentators have robbed his thought of any claim to originality. Moreover, by considering these influences in terms of clearly demarcated stages, they give the impression that his thought proceeded in a staccatolike manner, undergoing drastic changes at every start of a new influence as the Greek writer first abandoned an old mentor and then embraced a new one. They consequently see his thought as lacking the wholeness and continuity it actually has.

While we have to admit that the figures and the philosophies he himself often acknowledged did have an influence in formulating his thought, none of them was completely adopted by Kazantzakis nor was any of them completely abandoned. It is closer to the truth to say that each of these philosophies was assimilated by Kazantzakis' mind and was transformed in accordance with that mind's own chemistry to form a world view that was uniquely his own. In this sense aspects of each of these philosophies remained with him to the end of his life. This holds true of Buddhism, Bergsonism, Nietzscheanism, as well as of Marxism.

It would be just as misleading, therefore, to speak of the writer's Marxist or "left-wing stage" as it would be to speak of his Buddhist, nihilist stages, etc. And this notwithstanding his own assertion in a letter that "From 1923 to 1933 approximately . . . I belonged to the left wing."[57] Nor would it be completely correct, focusing on that ten-year period, to see it as one in which Kazantzakis' original hopes and embrace of communism in the early 1920s gradually dwindled, reaching a point of disillusionment which by the early 1930s forced his gaze away toward "metacommunism."

His notion of "metacommunism" was with him from the very beginning of that period. In fact, this concept first emerged along with his *Spiritual Exercises* which he finished in April, 1923, at the very time he was speaking so fervently about Russia. Again, that his outlook did not change and that he considered Russian communism as part of the transitional stage at the end as well as at the beginning of the "left wing" period, while he was still in Germany, has been attested to by the letters to his first wife. As early as 1923 he spoke of it in terms of "the middle ages." The same idea is stated in his "The Social Problem,"[58] published in February 1925. Finally, no such thing as disillusionment took place in him because, from the outset, long before his trip to Russia and amidst his enthusiastic letters, he wrote to his wife in 1922 that he "had not the slightest *illusion* about the present reality in Russia."

Ultimately, there are two ways that this period affected Kazantzakis. First, it brought him to the clear realization that he was not a man of concrete action, a realization which was to be forced on him once again in 1945 when as minister he tried to bring together the various Greek Socialist factions into one party. Secondly, because he witnessed, and to some extent partook of the Communist reality, this period afforded him the opportunity to formulate communism's significance and to articulate the various aspects of that significance in regard to human history and to man. In other words, it gave him the chance to clarify and formulate those ideas which he had, perhaps too abruptly, expressed in his letters early in that period. His stance in regard to that reality and the metaphysics on which it was based never substantially changed during that period, nor during any other period to the end of his life. We have already seen his criticism of theoretical Marxism. His objection that the fundamental metaphysical contentions of Marxism are one-sided and dogmatic, and his attitudes toward the unending faith of orthodox Communists, whom he considered naive, remained with him to the very end and explain why his books were banned in Russia. At the same time, however, his deep antipathy toward the decadent values of capitalism, his growing aversion toward imperialism and colonialism, his view that communism was the single reality defining the times, a reality which will have to be traversed if man is to be ushered into a new and higher era—all these convictions which admittedly grew during that "left wing" period were not abandoned with that period but persisted and solidified in the years to come, as his activities and writing show. And, of course, they were the reason for his being persecuted by every single rightist government in Greece.

In 1944, immediately after a period of isolation on the island of Aegina, he joined the democratic, Socialist, and resistance groups which had surfaced soon after the war. In May 1945, he was elected the first president of the SEE-Socialistiki Ergatiki Enosi (Socialist Labor Union). The same year he became Minister without portfolio—a position which he resigned a few months later. In the summer of 1946, while in England, a plebiscite brought back the king of Greece. In the fall, he moved to France. He was never to see Greece again.

Between the first and second civil wars in Greece, Kazantzakis became one of the few bearers of a Greek Socialist democratic ideology. Both as leader of the "Socialist Labor Union" and as minister, in speeches and announcements and press conferences, he put forth a Socialist political ideology whose roots went directly and undeniably back to his views of "The Social Problem" of 1925 and to his "Apology." He repeated the significance of the historical moment humanity was passing through, the necessity of destroying the molds of the old bourgeois civilization, the need to struggle for man's development; he insisted that such development is grounded not merely in economic emancipation but in the emancipation of the "light that exists within every man and every people. . . ."[59] "Only on psychological foundations can a civilization be solidified. The economic and political life is always regulated by a progress of man's soul."[60] To the end of his life he remained true to what in the early 1920s he had called his new development—his awakening to internationalism. From their very beginning he favored the anti-colonial revolutions which were breaking out in the aftermath of World War II, and he later became a supporter of the first and second international conferences which were being organized in Athens to prepare the grounds for the First International Anti-colonial Congress. It is the equality, cooperation, and freedom of the world's people that he spoke of when he addressed, a few months before his death, the International Peace Committee, on the occasion of his receiving the Peace Award in Vienna. In a passage whose resemblance to the letters of the early 1920s is undeniable, he states:

> One world staggers, ready to fall, another is being raised. Countless are the forms of destruction and reconstruction which are all around us. That is why man's responsibility is great today. He has realized that any one of his actions may affect the whole human destiny. He knows that men, black, white, yellow, are one. [If] at the other end of the world someone is hungry, we are to blame; we cannot be free if at the end of the world someone still remains a slave.[61]

Disillusioned with practical politics, discouraged by the attitudes of the great powers, embittered by the situation in Greece, which was "groaning under the Fascist yoke," self-exiled in southern France, Kazantzakis turned to that labor with which he was most at home; he turned, this time resolutely, to his literary activity. With the exception of *Zorba the Greek,* all of his great novels date from this time on. His writing of the novels however, should not be seen as an aesthetic diversion on his part. It neither brought an end to his role as an enlightener of the people nor did it mean the abandonment of those Marxist ideas which he had all along deemed progressive. As a novelist, he channeled those ideas through the medium of art, embodying them in the heroes and situations of his novels. The abstract statements of his travel books, letters, and all the other documents we have considered became concretized and enfleshed in the dramas of his stories.

As early as in his "Apology" we have seen him state that he took it to be his duty to articulate a clear idea of the historical moment we were passing through by enlightening the people and giving a new and loftier content to the conceptions of work, justice, and virtue. In his novels his protagonists Christ, Saint Francis, Manolios, Father Fotis, and Father Yanaros became the concrete embodiments of that higher moment we were going through in terms of a struggle whereby one civilization is about to fall and another about to begin. This struggle is concretely and passionately presented in the *Greek Passion* and *The Fratricides* in the struggle between those who believe that "the word rests on four pillars—religion, country, honor, and property"[62]—and those for whom such a world is "unjust and wicked . . . and must perish."[63] We need only to read these two novels to be convinced that Kazantzakis was neither bourgeois, Fascist, red, or immoral. His works suffice to contradict the claim that he was an egomaniac, oblivious to the fate of others. For in them, as in all his books, what Kazantzakis did is what he himself professed:

> I compel myself in my work to set heroic models before the people, not fictitious heroes who never existed, but those who have emerged from the vitals of my race. They alone incarnate the claims and the hopes of the famished and the persecuted and are capable of showing the people the way to salvation.[64]

That salvation, Kazantzakis was convinced, could not be found within the capitalist world. And if, as he was equally convinced, communism did not afford us the new beginning, at least it was the end of an era beyond which an opening of a new path could, however vaguely, be envisioned.

Bibliography

Engels, Friederick. *Ludwig Feuerback and the Outcome of Classical German Philosophy,* edited and translated by C.P. Dutt. New York: International Publishers Co., n.d.

Kazantzakis, Helen. *Nikos Kazantzakis: A Biography,* translated by A. Mims. New York: Simon and Schuster, 1968.

Kazantzakis, Nikos. *The Greek Passion,* translated by J. Griffin. New York: Simon and Schuster, 1953.

Kazantzakis, Nikos. *Toda Raba,* translated by A. Mims. New York: Simon and Schuster, 1964.

Panichas, George, Ed. *The Politics of Twentieth-Century Novelists.* New York: Hawthorne Books, Inc., 1971.

Prevelakis, Pandelis. *Nikos Kazantzakis and His Odyssey: A Study of the Poet and the Poem,* translated by P. Sherrard. New York: Simon and Schuster, 1961.

Notes

Chapter 1.

Léon Blum and
Democratic Socialism in France

1. On Blum's early life and activity, see Joel Colton, *Léon Blum: Humanist in Politics* (New York: Knopf, 1966), pp. 3-35. Geoffrey Fraser and Thadée Natanson, *Léon Blum: Man and Statesman* (Philadelphia: Lippincott, 1938), had much information on Blum's personal life. Natanson was one of Blum's old friends.

2. On Jean Jaurès, see Harvey Goldberg, *The Life of Jean Jaurès* (Madison: University of Wisconsin Press, 1962).

3. On Blum's activity in the Dreyfus Case, see Léon Blum, *Souvenirs sur l'Affaire* (Paris: Gallimard, 1935).

4. Léon Blum, *Les Nouvelles conversations de Goethe avec Eckermann*, as cited in *L'Oeuvre de Léon Blum, 1895-1901* (Paris: Albin Michel, 1954), I, p. 243.

5. On French Socialism before World War I, see Aaron Noland, *The Founding of the French Socialist Party, 1893-1905* (Cambridge: Harvard University Press, 1956).

6. For an excellent account of Blum's literary activities and works, see Richard L. Stokes, *Léon Blum: Poet to Premier* (New York: Coward McCann, 1937), chapters vi and vii.

7. Blum, *Souvenirs sur l'Affaire*, p. 75.

8. Paul Louis, *Histoire du socialisme en France de la Révolution à nos jours, 1789-1936* (Paris: Marcel Rivière, 1936), p. 336.

9. Goldberg, *Jean Jaurès*, p. 464.

10. Léon Blum, *La Réforme gouvernementale*, 2d ed. (Paris: B. Grasset, 1936), p. 120.

11. Ibid., p. 120.

12. Ibid., pp. 16-17.

13. Fraser and Natanson, *Léon Blum*, p. 142, and Stokes, *Léon Blum*, chapter x.

14. For a list of the twenty-one demands, see Louis, *Histoire du socialisme*, pp. 389-90.

15. Colette Audry, *Léon Blum ou la politique du juste* (Paris: René Julliard, 1955), p. 42.

171

16. Léon Blum, *Bolchevisme et socialisme,* 9th ed. (Paris: Librarie Populaire, 1937), p. 9. An excellent account of the differences between Blum's socialism and communism is in Annie Kriegel, *Aux Origines du Communisme français, 1914-1920,* 2 vols. (Paris: Mouton, 1964), vol. 2, pp. 791-811. For additional information on the French Communist Party, see Gerard Walter, *Histoire du parti communiste français* (Paris: Smogy, 1948).

17. *Bolchevisme et solcialisme,* p. 39.

18. Ibid., p. 8.

19. Ibid., p. 6.

20. Louis, *Histoire du socialisme,* p. 412.

21. On the French Radical party, see Peter J. Larmour, *The French Radical Party in the 1930's* (Palo Alto, Calif.: Stanford University Press, 1964).

22. For a good account on the Fascist leagues and the rioting on February 6, 1934, see Alexander Werth, *France in Ferment* (London: Harper and Brothers, 1934), pp. 142-75 and 265-81.

23. See John T. Marcus, *French Socialism in the Crisis Years, 1933-1936: Fascism and the French Left* (New York: Praeger, 1958), pp. 46-69 and 85-86.

24. For an extensive examination of Communist tactics vis-à-vis the French Popular Front, see Franz Borkenau, *European Communism* (New York: Harper and Brothers, 1953), chapter iv.

25. Colton, *Léon Blum,* pp. 102-3.

26. Ibid., pp. 111-13.

27. For a good account of the strikes, see Alexander Werth, *The Twilight of France, 1933-1940* (New York: Harper and Brothers, 1942), pp. 92-98; and Henry W. Ehrmann, *French Labor: From Popular Front to Liberation* (New York: Oxford University Press, 1947), pp. 38-40.

28. Léon Blum, *L'Exercise du pouvoir* (Paris: Gallimard, 1937), pp. 83-97.

29. Stokes, *Léon Blum,* pp. 231-41.

30. Ehrmann, *French Labor,* p. 84.

31. Colton, *Léon Blum,* p. 162.

32. On economic aspects and problems of the first Blum ministry, see Ehrmann, *French Labor,* pp. 60-76.

33. Colton, *Léon Blum,* pp. 270-76.

34. A plethora of material on Blum and Riom Trials is found in *L'Oeuvre de Léon Blum, 1940-1945* (Paris: Albin Michel, 1955), V, pp. 141-404.

35. Léon Blum, *A l'echelle humaine,* in *L'Oeuvre de Léon Blum,* V, pp. 409-95.

36. Ibid., p. 491.

37. *L'Oeuvre de Léon Blum, 1945-1947* (Paris: Albin Michel, 1958), VI. pp. 105-12.
38. Ibid., pp. 36-44.
39. Ibid, p. 283.
40. Ibid., p. 70.
41. Ibid., pp. 271-75.
42. For an excellent account of Blum's Socialist thought, see Joel Colton, "The French Socialist Party: A Case Study of the Non-Communist Left," *Yale Review* 43 (March, 1954): 402-13.
43. On French nationalization and social welfare after World War II, see Vsevolod Holubnychy and Alfred Oxenfeldt, *Economic Systems in Action: The United States, The Soviet Union, France* (New York: Holt, Rinehart, and Winston, 1966).

Salvador Allende:

Chile's Socialist President

1. Regis Debray, *The Chilean Revolution: Conversations with Allende* (New York: Vintage Books, 1971), p. 64.
2. Salvador Allende, *La realidad médico-social Chilena* (Santiago: n.p., 1939), p. 8.
3. Paul W. Drake, "The Chilean Socialist Party and Coalition Politics, 1932-1946," *The Hispanic American Historical Review* 53, no. 4 (November, 1973). 638-39.
4. See Jack Thomas, "An Expression of Latin American Socialist Views on World War II: The First Congress of the Democratic Parties of Latin America," *Social Science* 44, no. 3 (June, 1969). 145-53.
5. Raul Ampuero to Luis Corvalan, *Socialist Party Restates Its Disagreements with the Communist Party* (Santiago, April 9, 1960).
6. Salomon Corbalan Gonzáles, *Partido Socialista* (Concepción: In Academia de las Escuelas de Ciencias Políticas y Administrativas de las Universidades de Chile y de Concepción, 1957), pp. 8-24.
7. Salvador Allende, *Primer mensaje del presidente Allende ante el congreso pleno, 21 de Mayo de 1971* (Santiago: Talleres Gráficos Servicio de Prisones, 1971), pp. vi-ix.
8. Salvador Allende, *Chile's Road to Socialism* (Baltimore: Penguin Books, 1973), p. 57.
9. Ibid., p. 172.
10. Ibid., p. 55.
11. Ibid., pp. 57-61.
12. Ibid., p. 134.
13. Ibid., p. 94.
14. José Ortega y Gasset, *The Modern Theme* (New York: Harper and Row, 1961), p. 101.

[15] Allende, *Primer mensaje*, pp. v-xiii.
[16] Allende, *Chile's Road to Socialism*, p. 109.
[17] "The Popular Unity Program, 1969," reprinted in R. E. Feinberg, *The Triumph of Allende: Chile's Legal Revolution* (New York: New American Library, 1972), pp. 259-73.
[18] Allende, *Chile's Road to Socialism*, pp. 171-72.
[19] Peter Camejo, *Allende's Chile: Is It Going Socialist?* (New York: Pathfinder Press, 1971), p. 4.
[20] Salvador Allende, *Nuestro camino al socialismo* (Buenos Aires: Ediciones Papiro, 1971), p. 19.
[21] Ibid., p. 120.
[22] Richard Gott, "Military coup ends Chile's Marxism," *Manchester Guardian* 109, no. 11 (week ending September 15, 1973): 3.
[23] In a Havana speech, Castro quoted from this letter which he sent to Allende, July 29, 1973. Speech reprinted in Fidel Castro and Beatriz Allende, *Homenaje a Salvador Allende* (Habana, Cuba: Editorial Galerna, 1973), pp. 64-67.
[24] "Comment," *Manchester Guardian* 109, no. 13 (week ending September 29, 1973): 10.
[25] Camejo, *Allende's Chile*, pp. 8-10.
[26] Richard A. Gott, "Introduction," in Allende, *Nuestro camino al socialismo*, p. 18.
[27] Camejo, *Allende's Chile*, p. 13.

Chapter 2.

Jean Grave and
French Anarchism

[1] André Malraux, *Les Conquérants* (Paris: Bernard Grasset, 1928), p. 33.
[2] On Grave's life and ideas, see Louis Patsouras, *Jean Grave and French Anarchism* (Dubuque, Iowa: Kendall Hunt, 1978).
[3] Jean Grave, *La Grande famillé; roman militaire* (Paris: P.V. Stock, 1907) pp. 84-85.
[4] In the 1850s and 1860s, low wages which, with few exceptions, did not rise and an eleven-hour workday were the lot of the Parisian proletariat. On these and other social conditions, see Georges Duveau, *La Vie Ouvrière en France sous le Second Empire* (Paris: Gallimard, 1946).
[5] Ibid., p. 87.
[6] The influence of the 1871 Paris Commune on Grave's anarchism is unquestionable. For example, see Jean Grave, "Les Anarchistes sont les seuls socialistes," *Les Temps Nouveaux*, September 28-October 4, 1895, p. 1.
[7] Grave, *La Grande familie*, p. 183.
[8] Ibid., p. 197.

9. Ibid., pp. 131-35.

10. Ibid., pp. 190-92.

11. On French anarchism in the 1880 to 1914 period, the definitive work is Jean Maitron's *Historie du mouvement anarchiste en France* (1880-1914) (Paris: Société Universitaire d'Éditions et de Librarie, 1955).

12. On *Le Révolté, La Révolte* and *Les Temps Nouveaux,* see Maitron, *Historie,* and Patsouras, *Jean Grave.*

13. On Grave's literary work, see Patsouras, *Jean Grave.*

14. On Anarchist division vis-à-vis World War I, see Maitron, *Historie.*

15. Ibid.

16. On the decline of French anarchism after World War I, see Maitron, *Historie;* and Patsouras, *Jean Grave.*

17. On Anarchist theory and development, see the brilliant works: George Woodcock, *Anarchism: A History of Libertarian Ideas and Movements* (Cleveland: Meridian Books, 1962), and James Joll, *The Anarchists,* (New York: Universal Library, 1966).

18. The great work by Jean Grave criticizing bourgeois society is *La Société mourante et l'anarchie* (Paris: Tresse et Stock, 1893). See, for example, the attack on bourgeois imperialism and racism, pp. 17-97.

19. On Grave and revolution, including the reformist-revolutionary pattern, see Jean Grave, *La Société future* (Paris: P.V. Stock, 1895) and Jean Grave, *Réformes révolution* (Paris: V.P. Stock, 1910). Also, Patsouras, *Jean Grave,* for an analytical discussion of these problems. Grave's pattern for revolution is not essentially different than the Marxian one (both envisage the rise of socialism from a mass movement embracing the majority of the people): see Karl Marx and Friedrich Engels, *Manifesto of the Communist Party* (New York: International Publishers, 1948), pp. 9-19 and 29-31.

20. On the Marxian two-phased pattern for the realization of communism, see Karl Marx, *Critique of the Gotha Programme; With Appendices by Marx, Engels, Lenin,* edited by C.P. Dutt (New York: International Publishers, 1938).

21. For a detailed view of a practical Anarchist society, see Grave, *La Société future* and Jean Grave, *Terre Libre* (Les Pionniers) (Paris: Les Temps Nouveaux, 1908).

22. For criticism by Grave and others of Communist Russia, see various articles in Grave's Journal, *Publications de "La Révolte" et "Temps Nouveaux."*

23. On revolutionary syndicalism in France, see Edouard Dolléans, *Histore du mouvement oviér, 1871-1920* (Paris: Armand Colin, 1950). On the great theorist of revolutionary syndicalism, see

Richard Humphrey, *Georges Sorel, Prophet without Honor: A Study in Anti-Intellectualism* (Cambridge: Harvard University Press, 1951).

24. On Grave's theoretical differences with the Revolutionary Syndicalists, see Grave, *Réformes, révolution*, pp. 222-23.

25. On Grave's close relations with various Revolutionary Syndicalists, see Patsouras, *Jean Grave*.

26. On anarchism and art in which Grave's significance as a pioneer is recognized, see Eugenia W. Herbert, *The Artist and Social Reform: France and Belgium, 1885-1898* (New Haven: Yale University Press, 1961).

27. Ibid., and Patsouras, *Jean Grave*.

28. On the 1968 revolution, see Adrien Dansette, *Mai 1968* (Paris: Plon, 1971). Jean Maitron, "Anarchisme," *Le Mouvement Social* 69 (Oct.-Dec., 1969), p. 109, saw Anarchist ideas and inspiration as of primary importance in the 1968 revolution. A significant article on the importance of Anarchist ideas in the 1968 revolution is by Richard Gombin, "The Ideology and Practice of Contestation Seen through Recent Events in France," *Anarchism Today*, ed. by D. E. Apter and J. Joll (Garden City, N.Y.: Doubleday, 1971), pp. 14-33.

Chapter 3.
Georgi Dimitrov and the United, Popular, and National Fronts

1. Joseph Rothschild, *The Communist Party of Bulgaria: Origins and Development, 1883-1936* (New York: Columbia University Press, 1959) pp. 2, 51; Magdalina Barumova, *Spomeni za Georgi Dimitrov* [Remembrances of Georgi Dimitrov] (Sofia: Narodna Mladezh, 1963), pp. 10, 22-23. Barumova was Dimitrov's sister. Translation from Bulgarian.

2. Ibid., p. 52.

3. William Vettes, "The 1903 Schism of the Bulgarian Social Democracy and the Second International," *American Slavic and East European Review*, Dec. 1960, pp. 521, 523; M. A. Birman, "Tesnyaki i rukovodstvo II Internationala" [The Narrows and the Leadership of the Second International], *Uchenye Zapiski Instituta Slavyanovedeniia*, vol. 30, p. 172. Translated from Russian.

4. Ibid., pp. 172-73.

5. Ibid., p. 174; Rothschild, *Communist Party*, pp. 52-53.

6. Vettes, "1903 Schism," pp. 521, 528.

7. Elena Savova, *Georgi Dimitrov: letopis na zhivota i revoliutsionnata mu deinost* [Georgi Dimitrov: A Chronicle of His Life and Revolutionary Activities] (Sofia: Bulgarian Academy of Sciences, 1952) pp. 16-18, 24, 73-74. Translated from Bulgarian.

8. Ibid., pp. 31, 38, 41, 61-62, 64, 79, 85, 91, 100, 119, 134-35.

9. Birman, "Tesnyaki," pp. 179-85.

10. Boris Yanovski "Naroden tribun i obshchestven deets" [Popular Tribune and Social Activist] *Slavyani* 28, 6, pp. 24-26. Translation from Bulgarian.

11. Rothschild, *Communist Party*, p. 54; Kosta Todorov *Balkan Firebrand* (New York: Davis-Zipf, 1943) pp. 101-2.

12. Rothschild, *Communist Party*, pp. 74, 78, 81-82.

13. Ibid., p. 82, 87-88, 93, 97-98, Todorov, *Balkan Firebrand,* pp. 131-32.

14. Franz Borkenau, *European Communism* (New York: Harper, 1953) pp. 238-40; Rothschild, *Communist Party,* pp. 105, 110.

15. Borkenau, *European Communism,* pp. 240-41; Rothschild, *Communist Party,* pp. 121-23.

16. Savova, *Georgi Dimitrov,* pp. 332-33, 338-39.

17. Ibid., p. 330.

18. Ibid., p. 340.

19. F. T. Konstantinov, "Tvorcheskaia razrabotka nekotorykh voprosov Marksistsko-Leninskoi teorii v trudakh G. M. Dimitrova" [The Creative Solution of Some Problems of Marxist-Leninist Theory in the Writings of G. M. Dimitrov], *Institut Slavyanovedeniia* vol. 24, pp. 21-22. Translation from Russian.

20. Nissan Oren, "Popular Fronts in the Balkans: Bulgaria," *Journal of Contemporary History* 5, no. 3: 73; Borkenau, *European Communism,* p. 241.

21. P. P. Radenkova, "Georgi Dimitrov: revoliutsionner-internationalist," *Voprosy istorii* 42, no. 9 (1967), pp. 131-32. Translation from Russian.

22. Todorov, *Balkan Firebrand,* pp. 200, 203-5.

23. A. N. Kirshevskaia, "Pravitel'stvo Stamboliskogo v Bolgarii (1919-1923," [The Stamboliskii Regime in Bulgaria, 1919-1923], *Institut Slavyanovedeniia* vol. 12, p. 51. Translation from Russian.

24. Radenkova, "Georgi Dimitrov," p. 133.

25. Ibid., pp. 135-36.

26. Oren, "Popular Fronts," p. 74; Stela Dimitrova, *Moskovskoto suveshtanie na B.K.P., 1925* [The Moscow Conference of the Bulgarian Communist Party, 1925] (Sofia: Bulgarian Communist Party, 1959), pp. 7-8, 29, 34, 57-58. Translation from Bulgarian.

27. Ibid., pp. 59-62, 96.

28. Ibid., p. 77; Radenkova, "Georgi Dimitrov," pp. 136-38.

29. Ibid., p. 138. Boyan Grigorov, *B.K.P. prez perioda na vremennata i chastichna stabilizatsiia na kapitalizma* [The Bulgarian Communist Party During the Period of the Temporary and Partial Stabilization of Capitalism, 1925-1929] (Sofia: Bulgarian Communist Party, 1961) p. 111. Translation from Bulgarian.

30. Ibid., pp. 61-79, 83-84. Dimitrov declared with emotion: "Please

let me say a few words about myself. I have been on the Central Committee continuously since 1909. I bear responsibility for all the errors of the Central Committee. . . . The June 9 debacle weighs upon me like Mont Blanc, and will burden me to my grave. That was an error of opportunism from beginning to end" (p. 77).

31. Oren, "Popular Fronts," pp. 74-75.

32. Rothschild, *Communist Party*, pp. 288-92; Savova, *Georgi Dimitrov*, pp. 267-372.

33. Jane Degras (ed.) *The Communist International, 1919-1943: Documents* (London: Frank Case, 1971), 3, p. 239; Babette Gross, *Willi Munzenberg: A Political Biography* (Ann Arbor: University of Michigan Press, 1974), pp. 240, 251.

34. Barumova, *Spomeni*, p. 68; Savova, *Georgi Dimitrov*, pp. 388-409.

35. Ibid., p. 409; Nissan Oren, *Bulgarian Communism: The Road to Power, 1934-1944* (New York: Columbia University Press, 1971), p. 99; Babette Gross, "The German Communists' United Front and Popular Front Venture," in M. Drachkovitch and B. Lazitch (eds.), *The Comintern: Historical Highlights* (New York: Praeger, 1966), p. 120.

36. Eudocia Ravines, *The Yenan Way* (New York: Charles Scribner's Sons, 1951), pp. 113-14. His impression was that the Russian Dimitri Manuilsky, reflecting Stalin's caution and suspicions, blocked Dimitrov from leading the Comintern into a Popular Front policy in 1934. See pp. 145-46 and Degras, *The Communist International*, p. 333.

37. Kermit McKenzie, *The Comintern and World Revolution, 1928-1943* (New York: Columbia University Press, 1964) pp. 30, 43, 144, 152-53.

38. Degras, *The Communist International*, pp. 153-54.

39. McKenzie, *The Comintern*, pp. 153-54.

40. Ibid., pp. 155, 158-59, 196, 332, 337.

41. Milorad Drachkovitch. "The Comintern and the Insurrectional Activity of the Communist Party of Yugoslavia, 1941-1942," in Drachkovitch and Lazitch, *The Comintern*, pp. 185, 195, 212-13.

42. Stoiko Kolev, *Borbata na B.K.P. za naroden front, 1935-1939* [Struggle of the Bulgarian Communist Party for a Popular Front, 1935-1939] (Sofia: Bulgarian Communist Party, 1959), pp. 125-30, 147-48, 177-78; Oren, "Popular Fronts," pp. 76-81.

43. Savova, *Georgi Dimitrov*, pp. 481-83; Oren, *Bulgarian Communism*, p. 99.

44. Konstantinov, "Tvorcheskaia," pp. 23-24.

45. Georgi Kulishev, vice-president of the National Assembly, interviewed in *Slavyani* 28, no. 1, p. 30; Krustio Goranov, "Georgi Dimitrov i sotsialisticheskata kultura" [Georgi Dimitrov and Socialist Culture] *Slavyani* 28, no. 6, pp. 20-21; Savova, *Georgi Dimitrov*, pp. 501, 518, 566.

Bac Ho:

Ho Chi Minh of Vietnam

1. Bac Ho, meaning "Uncle Ho," was the term of affection by which the people of Vietnam referred to Ho Chi Minh, which in the Vietnamese language means "He Who Enlightens."

2. The OSS was the World War II forerunner of the Central Intelligence Agency (CIA), gathering, on behalf of the United States, information regarding German, Italian, and Japanese military activities.

3. Charles Fenn, *Ho Chi Minh: A Biographical Introduction* (New York: Charles Scribner's Sons, 1973), p. 132.

4. Bernard Fall, *Last Reflections on a War* (New York: Schoken Books, 1972), p. 59.

5. Nguyen Sinh Cung had, as we shall see, as many pseudonyms as Lon Chaney had faces.

6. The French colony of Indochina consisted of five territories: Tonkin in the north; Annam in the central strip along the coast of the Gulf of Tonkin; Cochin China in the southeast; Cambodia to the southwest; and Laos, north of Cambodia and west of present-day Vietnam. In the late 1700s, the Emperior Gia-Long unified Tonkin, Annam, and Cochin China under the name of Vietnam. When the French conquered Vietnam they redivided it into the three regions and called all the inhabitants of each region *Annamese.*

7. The mandarin service, or Mandarinate, was a civil service system borrowed from Chinese culture. To enter the imperial officialdom and thus become a Mandarin, one had to pass "competitive examinations of an academic and cultural nature."

8. Hoang Van Chi, *From Colonialism to Communism: A Case History of North Vietnam* (New York: Praeger, 1964), pp.36f., claims that Ho's father was arrested and sent to Poulo Condore, a brutal penal colony in the Indian Ocean.

9. Fall, *Last Reflections,* p. 63. Fall reports that Vietnamese historians say young Ho was dismissed for his politics while his teachers claimed his expulsion from school was the result of his "poor grades." It is difficult to believe the latter claim in view of the fact that, among Ho's many talents and intellectual skills, he "spoke Vietnamese, French, English, Russian, Siamese and at least three Chinese dialects, in addition to having a working knowledge of several other languages." Fenn, *Ho Chi Minh,* p. 19.

10. Perhaps Ho adopted a new name because he was already listed by the French as a troublemaker. "Ba" (Three) was a logical pseudonym, since he was the third child in his family.

11. Wilfred Burchett, *Ho Chi Minh: An Appreciation* (New York: The Guardian, 1972), p. 9.

12. Ho Chi Minh, *Ho Chi Minh on Revolution: Selected Writings, 1920-1966* (New York: Praeger, 1967), p. vii.
13. Burchett, *Ho Chi Minh*, p. 9.
14. Ho Chi Minh, *Ho Chi Minh on Revolution*, p. viii. This attitude took some time in developing. At one point in the 1920s, Ho used the name Nguyen O Phap (Nguyen Who Hates the French) for which he was chastised by the French Communist party specialist on colonial affairs.
   Ho Chi Minh, "The Path Which Led Me to Leninism," in Jack Woodis, *Selected Articles and Speeches of Ho Chi Minh, 1920-1967* (London: Lawrence and Wishart Ltd., 1969), p. 156.
16. Ibid.
17. Ibid., p. 157.
18. Bui Lam quoted in Jean Chesneaux, *Days with Ho Chi Minh* (Hanoi: Foreign Languages Publishing House, 1965), p. 46.
19. Nguyen Ai Quoc, *La Correspondence Internationale*, German edition, no. 46, 1924, cited in N. Khac Huyen, *Vision Accomplished?: The Enigma of Ho Chi Minh* (New York: Macmillan, 1971), p. 12.
20. Ai Quoc quoted in Fall, *Last Reflections*, p. 72.
21. Longuet led the right wing in forming another Socialist party within the Second International.
22. N. Khac Huyen, *Vision Accomplished?*, pp. 17-18.
23. Fenn, *Ho Chi Minh*, p. 56, n. 23.
24. Ibid., p. 57.
25. Fall, *Last Reflections*, p. 79.
26. The Japanese invasion of China in 1937 forced Chiang Kai-shek to join forces (uneasily) with the Chinese Communists in order to fight the invaders. It was then possible for Tran to enter China without fear of the Kuomintang.
27. Tran quoted in Pham Van Dong and the Committee for the Study of the History of the Vietnamese Workers' Party, *Our President: Ho Chi Minh* (Hanoi: Foreign Languages Publishing House, 1970), p. 114.
28. Fenn, *Ho Chi Minh*, p. 68.
29. Government statement quoted in *Ibid.*, p. 89.
30. Ibid.
31. Woodis, *Selected Articles and Speeches*, p. 11.
32. Pham Van Dong, *Our President*, pp. 123-24.
33. Ibid., p. 11.
34. Appeal of the Party's Central Committee in Ibid., pp. 184-85.
35. Ibid., p. 205.
36. Chesneaux, *Days with Ho Chi Minh*, 174-75.
37. Burchette, *Ho Chi Minh*, p. 30.
38. Ibid., p. 30.
39. N. Khac Huyen, *Vision Accomplished?* p. 316.

40. Burchette, *Ho Chi Minh,* p. 27.
41. Quoted by Paul Mus, *Vietnam: Sociologie d'une Guerre* in Fenn, *Ho Chi Minh,* p. 39.
42. Burchette, *Ho Chi Minh,* p. 25.
43. Ibid., p. 30.
44. Ho Chi Minh, "Last Testament," quoted in Pham Van Dong, *Our President,* p. 191.
45. Central Committee of the Vietnamese Workers' party, "Last Tribute," quoted in Pham Van Dong, *Our President,* p. 194.

Chapter 4.

Lucio Colletti on
Socialism and Democracy

1. See, for example the writings of Umberto Cerroni, Norberto Bobbio, and Galvano della Volpe.
2. Lucio Colletti, "A Political and Philosophical Interview," *New Left Review,* no. 86, July-August, 1974, p. 14; and Lucio Colletti, (ed.), introduction to Karl Marx, *Early Writings* (New York: n.p., 1975), p. 45.
3. Lucio Colletti, *From Rousseau to Lenin* (New York: Monthly Rev., 1972).
4. For Rousseau's definition of a republic, see Book 2, Chapter 6 of *The Social Contract,* (New York, 1947). For his definition of democracy see Book 3, Chapter 4. For his distinction between the legislative and executive branches, see Book 2, Chapter 7 and Book 3, Chapter 1. For his discussion of unanimous and majority decisions, see Book 4, Chapter 2. For the commitment to principles, see those sections dealing with the general will, especially Book 1, Chapters 6 and 8. For the importance of equality, see Book 2, Chapters 1 and 11.
5. Colletti, Introduction, Marx, *Early Writings,* pp. 28-46.
6. Ludwig Feuerbach, "Ueber das *Wesen des Christentums* in Beziehung auf den *Einzigen und sein Eigentum*" in Feuerbach, *Werke in sechs Banden,* vol. 4, (Frankfurt: n.p., 1975).
7. See Marx's *The Civil War in France* in Karl Marx, *The First International and After* (New York: n.p., 1974).
8. Ibid., pp. 345-46.
9. Ibid., p. 212.
10. Ibid., p. 210.
11. Ibid., pp. 208-12.
12. John Stuart Mill, *Representative Government* (New York: n.p., 1951), chapter 12.
13. Colletti, *From Rousseau to Lenin,* pp. 166-67.
14. See the chapter called "Of Real Property" in Rousseau, *The Social Contract* and the chapter called "Of Property" in Locke's *The*

Second Treatise of Government in John Locke, *Two Treatises of Government* (New York: n.p., 1965).
15. Colletti, *From Rousseau to Lenin,* pp. 45-108.
16. Ibid., p. 106.
17. Ibid., pp. 220-21.
19. Colletti, "A Political and Philosophical Interview," p. 23.
20. Lucio Colletti, "Gramsci and Revolution," *New Left Review,* no. 65, January-February, 1971.
28. Ibid., p. 107.
21. Ibid., p. 91.
22. Lucio Colletti, "The Question of Stalin," *New Left Review,* no. 61, May-June, 1970.
23. Colletti, "A Political and Philosophical Interview," pp. 27-28.

Chapter 5.

Humanistic Socialism:
Erich Fromm

1. Erich Fromm, *Escape from Freedom* (New York: Rinehart, 1941), p. 22.
2. Ibid., p. 19.
3. Ibid., p. 25.
4. Ibid., pp. 35-36.
5 Ibid., p. 140.
6. Ibid.
7. Ibid., p. 110.
8. Ibid., pp. 155-56.
9. Ibid., p. 158.
10. See Erich Fromm, *The Anatomy of Human Destructiveness* (New York: Holt, Rinehart and Winston, 1973).
11. Fromm, *Escape from Freedom,* p. 184.
12. Ibid., p. 206.
13. Ibid.
14. Ibid., p. 290.
15. Erich Fromm, *Man for Himself* (New York: Rinehart, 1947), p. 7.
16. Ibid.
17. Ibid., p. 59.
18. Ibid., p. 62.
19. Ibid., pp. 65-66.
20. Ibid., p. 84.
21. Ibid., p. 88.
22. Ibid., pp. 97-98.
23. Ibid.
24. Erich Fromm, *The Sane Society* (New York: Rinehart, 1955), p. 31.
25. Fromm, *Man for Himself,* pp. 144-45.

26. Ibid., p. 158.

27. See D. C. Hodges, *Socialist Humanism* (St. Louis: Warren H. Green, 1974).

28. Erich Fromm, *Marx's Concept of Man* (New York: Ungar, 1961), p. 262.

Chapter 6.

Marxism and Kazantzakis

1. In a letter dated Dec. 18, 1953 from Amsterdam, Kazantzakis complained to his intimate friend Pandelis Prevelakis that the Swedish Academy, responsible for the Nobel Prize, was being bombarded with letters by Greeks against him. In the same letter, he wrote that a representative of the Greek intellectuals had told the Swedish king and members of the Academy that "I am a Communist and corrupt Greek youth and that it would be a humiliation to Greece were my person honored with the Nobel Prize." Τετρακόσια γράμματα τοῦ Καζαντζάκη στό Πρεβελάκη ed. by Pandelis Prevelakis (Athens: n.p., 1965), p. 649.

2. Ἀναγέννηση, April 1928, p. 380.

3. From an article by Emi Sao in the *People's Daily*, Peking, vol. 21, 1957. Reprinted in Greek as "A Gentle Fighter," Καινούργια Ἐποχή Fall 1958, pp. 158-59.

4. See the incident related by Peter Bien in "Nikos Kazantzakis," *"The Politics of Twentieth-Century Novelists,* ed. by George Panichas (New York: Hawthorne Books, 1971), pp. 137-38.

5. Nikos D. Pouliopoulos, Ὁ Νίκος Καζαυτζάκης καί τά παγκόσμια ἰδεολογικά ρεύματα , vol. 1 (Athens: n.p., 1972), p. 17.

6. Prevelakis, Τετρακόσια γράμματα, p. 150.

7. Παρισινά γράμματα: Ἡ ἐξέγερσις τοῦ σοσιαλισμοῦ, Νέον Ἄστυ, Nov. 1907, reprinted in Νέα Εστία , 15 Aug. 1958, p. 12-13.

8. Ἐπιστολές πρός τήν Γαλάτεια (Athens: n.p., 1958), pp. 18-21.

9. Ibid., p. 39.

10. Ibid., p. 26.

11. Ibid., p. 34.

12. Ibid., p. 194.

13. Ibid., p. 78.

14. Ibid., p. 258.

15. Ibid., p. 138.

16. Ibid., pp. 201-2.

17. A translation of the "Apology" is appended at the end of *Nikos Kazantzakis: A Biography,* by Helen Kazantzakis, tr. by A. Mims (New York: Simon and Schuster, 1958), p. 566.

18. Ibid.

19. Ibid., p. 568.
20. Ibid., p. 569.
21. Nikos Kazantzakis, Ταξιδεύοντας: Ρουσία, 5th ed. (Athens: n.p., 1969), p. 68. It is important to note that Kazantzakis' impressions of Russia were first published in 1926 in articles for the Athenian newspaper Ελεύθερος Λόγος. These articles were subsequently published in two volumes entitled Τί είδα στή Ρουσία. Kazantzakis published the one volume edition entitled Ταξιδεύοντας: Ρουσία in 1928 soon after his return from his last trip to the Soviet Union.
22. Panait Istrati was a Greek-Romanian writer who was introduced to the literary world of France by Romain Rolland as the "Gorki of the Balkans" and who was loved by the European public for his stories about his own vagrant life. At the very height of his fame, we are told by Kazantzakis himself, "in one of his articles in L'Humanité, full of indignation and disgust, he bade farewell to Western civilization, rotting in dishonor and injustice, and took refuge, in a new land, where he could live and work—in Russia." Πρωΐα, Dec. 31, 1927.
23. See Helen Kazantzakis's "Afterword," in Nikos Kazantzakis, Toda Raba, tran. by A. Mims (New York: Simon and Schuster, 1964, p. 210. Brettakos, Ό Νίκος Καζαντζάκης: Ή 'αγωνία του καί τό έργο του (Athens: n.p., 1970), pp. 140-41.
24. Pandelis Prevelakis, Nikos Kazantzakis and His Odyssey: A Study of the Poet and the Poem, tr. by P. Sherrard (New York: Simon and Schuster, 1961), p. 136.
25. Both the deep temperamental differences between the two friends as well as Kazantzakis' views about the world in general and Russia in particular—views of which we will speak later and which had a negative influence on Istrati—helped bring about the crisis, and the abrupt end of Istrati's journey. See Kazantzakis' letters of that period in Τετρακόσια γράμματα. Aspects of Kazantzakis' discussions with Istrati on Russia and communism were dramatized in Toda Raba in the conversation between Geranos and Azad.
26. Nikos Kazantzakis and His Odyssey, Greek ed. (Athens: n.p., 1958), p. 322, note 245.
27. N. Kazantzakis, Toda Raba, p. 63. Conceived in his second trip to Russia, this book was first published in French in 1938.
28. Ibid., p. 120.
29. Ibid., p. 94.
30. H. Kazantzakis, Nikos Kazantzakis: A Biography, p. 135.
31. Kazantzakis, Toda Raba, p. 117.
32. Prevelakis, Nikos Kazantzakis and His Odyssey, p. 160.
33. N. Kazantzakis, Ρουσία , p. 338.
34. Prevelakis, Nikos Kazantzakis and His Odyssey, p. 129.
35. N. Kazantzakis, Toda Raba, p. 159.

36. Prevelakis,Τετρακόσια γράμματα, p. 156. We will have occasion to refer again to this essay. Written from Gottesgab in 1929, soon after his return from Russia, this document, together with the "Apology," as Prevelakis himself does not fail to note, is indispensable for becoming acquainted with Kazantzakis' position concerning Marxism.
37. Ibid., p. 154.
38. Ibid.
39. Ibid.,
40. Ibid., p. 151.
41. N. Kazantzakis, Ρουσία , pp. 222-23.
42. Ibid., p. 224.
43. Ibid., p. 225.
44. Ibid., p. 221.
45. Friederick Engels, *Ludwig Feuerbach and the Outcome of Classical German Philosophy*, ed. and tran. by C. P. Dutt (New York: International Publishers Co.), p. 12.
46. N. Kazantzakis, Ρουσία, pp. 218-29.
47. Ibid., p. 220.
48. Prevelakis, Τετροκόσια γράμματα , p. 153.
49. Ibid., p. 154.
50. Ibid.
51. H. Kazantzakis, *Nikos Kazantzakis: A Biography*, p. 567.
52. N. Kazantzakis, Ρουσία , p. 261.
53. Ibid., p. 269.
54. Prevelakis, Τετροκόσια γράμματα , p. 155.
55. Ibid.
56. Ibid.
57. Prevelakis, *Nikos Kazantzakis and His Odyssey*, p. 160.
58. Ὁ Καζαντζάκης μιλεῖ γιά θεό, ed. by K. Mitsotakis (Athens: n.p., 1965), pp. 126-33.
59. From a speech on the BBC on July 18, 1946. H. Kazantzakis, *Nikos Kazantzakis: A Biography*, p. 443.
60. Ibid.
61. Pouliopoulos, Ὁ Νίκος, p. 20
62. Nikos Kazantzakis, *The Greek Passion*, tr. by J. Griffin, (New York: Simon and Schuster, 1953), pp. 259-60.
63. Ibid., p. 422.
64. H. Kazantzakis, *Nikos Kazantzakis: A Biography*, p. 530.

Index